THE JAPANESE ECONOMIC CRISIS

WITHDRAWN

Also by Jon Woronoff

ASIA'S 'MIRACLE' ECONOMIES
HONG KONG: CAPITALIST PARADISE
INSIDE JAPAN, INC
JAPAN AS – *ANYTHING BUT* – NUMBER ONE
JAPAN: THE COMING ECONOMIC CRISIS
JAPAN: THE COMING SOCIAL CRISIS
JAPAN'S COMMERCIAL EMPIRE
JAPAN'S MARKET: THE DISTRIBUTION SYSTEM
   (*with Michael R. Czinkota*)
JAPAN'S WASTED WORKERS
* JAPANESE TARGETING
THE JAPAN SYNDROME
KOREA'S ECONOMY: MAN-MADE MIRACLE
THE 'NO-NONSENSE' GUIDE TO DOING BUSINESS
   IN JAPAN
ORGANIZING AFRICAN UNITY
* POLITICS: THE JAPANESE WAY
UNLOCKING JAPAN'S MARKETS
WEST AFRICAN WAGER: HOUPHOUET VERSUS
   NKRUMAH
WORLD TRADE WAR

* *Published by St. Martin's*

The Japanese Economic Crisis

Jon Woronoff
Correspondent
Asian Business

St. Martin's Press   New York

© Jon Woronoff 1992

First published in Japan by Yohan Publications Inc.
under the title *Japan: The (Coming) Economic Crisis* 1992
First published in the United States of America in 1993 by
St. Martin's Press

Printed in Great Britain

ISBN 0–312–10368–9

Library of Congress Cataloging-in-Publication Data
Woronoff, Jon.
The Japanese economic crisis / Jon Woronoff.
p.   cm.
First published in Japan under title: Japan—the (coming)
economic crisis.
Includes bibliographical references and index.
ISBN 0–312–10368–9
1. Japan—Economic conditions—1989–   2. Japan—Economic
conditions—1945–1989.   3. Economic forecasting—Japan.   I. Title.
HC462.95.W67   1993
330.952'04—dc20   93–26046
                                                              CIP

Contents

Foreword

1. The (Coming) Economic Crisis
What Is A Crisis? 11
When Is It Coming? 14
Ready Or Not 18

2. Economic Miracles and Mirages
No More Growth Hero 23
Unsteady As She Goes 28
What Went Wrong? 32
Excuses, Excuses 37

3. Economic Super-Management
Planning And Targeting, Sort Of 45
Financial Wizardry 50
Rearranging The Economy 54

4. The Little Train That Couldn't
The Mighty Locomotive 61
The Cumbersome Wagons 64
A Two-Track Economy 68

5. **Japan's Wasted Workers**
   Productivity Peters Out 75
   Contrast In Blue And White 79
   Japan's Renowned (Mis)management System 84
   Subsidies And Services 88
   Ballot Boxes And Red Tape 92

6. **Rich Nation, Poor People**
   Only Rich On Paper 99
   Profitless Companies 104
   Pity The Poor Worker............................110
   Let The Consumer Pay............................115
   Government-Induced Waste.......................120

7. **What Quality Of Life?**
   Of Rabbit Hutches.... 127
   And Workaholics 132
   Spiritual Want 137
   Old Age Insecurity..............................140

8. **The Human Element Fails**
   Eroding Work Ethic..............................149
   Decaying Loyalty 154
   Gaping Generation Gaps 160

9. **Work Is No Fun**
   The Company "Family" 169
   Blue-Collar Blues 174
   White-Collar Blahs..............................180
   Working Women's Woes 186

10. **Demise Of The Classless Society**
    New Rich, New Poor 195
    Whose Company Is This?........................204
    Birth Of An Aristocracy 212

11. The Crisis Cometh

So Far, No Good 219
What About The Future? 224
Rising, Setting Or Immobile? 228
Crime And Punishment 236

Bibliography 243
Index...249

Foreword

Well over a decade ago, I wrote the predecessor to this book, *Japan: The Coming Economic Crisis*. It was one of the most critical books by a foreigner on the Japanese economy then and for a long time to come. Yet, now that I am reviewing the economy again, I find that this new book is even more critical. The reasons for this are simple: the situation has gotten worse and, after an extra decade's study, I understand better how the economy works . . . or does not work, as the case may be.

Nowadays a book like this would be called "revisionistic." To deflect such labels, let me stress that I am not a revisionist. To the contrary, I am part of the only mainstream that counts, the Japanese mainstream. What I say here echoes what is said every day by Japanese economists, journalists, academics, politicians and ordinary people. That is why I take such pains to buttress my comments on those of Japanese authorities and, where they exist, public opinion polls.

These views are *only* revisionistic when compared to the babbling brook of foreign apologistic literature. In English, and increasingly in other languages, authors are diligently trying to convince the rest of the world that things in Japan are for the best. They go out of their way to praise every aspect of the Japanese economy, society and nation. Some actually believe this nonsense; most do it for the money. But, no matter what they may claim, they are the "revisionists." They are spreading views that few in Japan believe and many find perfectly absurd.

Obviously, since more than a decade has passed, it was necessary to refresh the old book. However, rather than merely update and refine, I opted for a complete rewrite. This is a completely new book and the only words that have been borrowed are in the titles and themes. But it will appear familiar to those who read the first crisis book, because the underlying ideas have not varied. Indeed, as noted, they have become sharper and more pointed with time.

Admittedly, not everything I said in my first attempt was correct and, wherever necessary, the material has been amended. But what surprises me is how much was on the mark. A decade ago, most of the critics thought I had gone too far. They assumed that, if ever I wrote a second edition, it would have to apologize abjectly for having underestimated those running the economy. Instead, as we all know, the economy has weakened and numerous aberrations and abuses have been uncovered. If anything, Japan has fared worse than they expected or I imagined.

Aside from the updating, correcting and refining, I have made another addition. It was essential to explain more exactly what a "crisis" is. Too many observers assume that it can only take the form of slower growth, so slow that the economy wilts. But many more things can go wrong than that. And, for most ordinary Japanese, the crisis has manifested itself in other ways that are described herein, ways we can all understand and would dislike if they affected us.

No matter how hard I try, I do not suppose I can convince the doubters, those who believe Japan's economy is truly miraculous. And it is impossible to persuade the professional apologists. But there are many others who can learn from this book, both foreigners and Japanese. After all, the first crisis book was very widely read and did play a crucial role in providing an alternative view and showing the other side of the Japanese "miracle" to those who wished to see. I hope this book and all my books will continue fulfilling that function.

I also hope my books will continue helping readers to understand the realities of Japan, realities they would not expect if they only read the rosier apologist literature. After all, events increasingly indicate that the Japanese system is not as good as advertised. Unpleasant, and to the unwary, inexplicable events have happened, like the bursting of the "bubble economy" or the collapse of the Liberal Democratic Party due to excessive corruption and refusal to reform. Something is clearly rotten in Japan and revealing it will do more good than concealing it.

JON WORONOFF

1
The (Coming) Economic Crisis

What Is A Crisis?

Looked at from a certain angle, Japan's economy is an extraordinary success. Just after the war, it only accounted for 1 percent of the world's gross national product. Now it exceeds 13 percent. Its growth has been unmatched by other advanced economies for over four decades, actually achieving 10 percent and more a year during its most vigorous period. Today, Japan is the leading producer of consumer electronics, semiconductors, steel, watches, ships, etc. and should add automobiles and computers to the list soon. Its products are admired worldwide and its exports reach every corner of the earth.

How can one possibly fault such a record? How can one go yet further and talk of a crisis, albeit one that is just coming?

Well, if economic growth is the only yardstick, then such criticism would be quite impossible. But, as all too many foreign observers forget, growth is not the only criterion of any economy. There are other ways of measuring success and they may not point in the same direction. In fact, they may detract from the initial impression of a brilliant success and actually lead one to question just what a success is.

One of the other yardsticks is whether the economy instills a sense of satisfaction among those who make it run. After all, there is a distinct difference between an economy which gives the economic actors a feeling of achievement and fulfillment and one that makes ordinary workers feel that they scarcely matter and are just doing the boss' bidding. It is not quite the same to follow a path that leads somewhere and walk on a treadmill that turns and turns without going anywhere.

More difficult to define, but even more significant, is whether the economy provides the population with what it wants. Most people do not work for the pure pleasure of working, not even in Japan. They expect some sort of reward. That often takes the form of a salary or other remuneration and is used to purchase those things the economic actors desire. Just how much they earn, expressed in purely monetary terms, is considerably less important than what they can buy with it. So the gains must be adjusted to purchasing power when comparisons are made.

Yet harder to define exactly is what standard of living can be achieved by the people. They want not only material goods, food, clothing, housing. They also want some leisure and enjoyment. They fancy an agreeable living environment, with adequate amenities and pleasant neighborhoods. They seek quality of life, undefinable in words but clearly sensed by those who do—or do not—possess it.

To this might be added comfort and security in their old age. Economies can be very powerful if they do not put aside the wherewithal to support the elderly and that would hardly be noticed for decades, until the time comes to pay the bill. It is thus necessary to ascertain whether Japan has made the essential investments in health and welfare, social security and old age pensions, clinics, old age homes and the personnel to staff them.

Finally, whether or not the economy has generated wealth

and provided security, there is still the question of whether any gains have been shared fairly and squarely. Once again, one can quibble over just what this means. Some will insist that the gains be shared equally among all while others think they should be divided in keeping with each person's contribution. Yet, whatever the preference, it is possible to check whether the bulk of the population, or those making the bulk of the effort, have gained reasonably or whether most of the gains have gone to a small group of haves leaving the have-nots worse off.

Of course, in all of the above, it is indispensable to consider another possibility. Perhaps the results appear better than they actually are because the statistics used to measure them are false. Maybe the yardstick is not true and measures more or less than a yard, depending on what the authorities prefer. As we all know, it is easy to lie with statistics and many Japanese statistics are particularly treacherous.

From this enumeration of different ways in which an economy can be evaluated, it must be obvious that it is *not* enough to talk of success just because an economy grows fast and produces a lot. It may still be an unpleasant one in which to work, creating a society with little quality of life and even less *joie de vivre*. It can be productive but not fruitful, failing to fulfill many of the intrinsic needs of the population. So, it is imperative to look more closely before coming to a conclusion, positive or negative.

And this is particularly applicable to Japan. For there is no other economy where the discrepancy between economic growth and what it brings the people is so great. That is because, as will be shown in greater detail in the following chapters, Japan is only first rate when it comes to growth. The economy rates much lower when measured by any of the other yardsticks mentioned. Indeed, it often turns out to be among the worse performers.

Even this would not be terribly serious if not for the fact

that the Japanese people place an ever higher priority on other aspects than growth. They clearly want shorter hours, increased wages and purchasing power, more leisure, larger homes, more abundant amenities, and more fun. They also want a greater degree of fairness in the distribution of wealth and, above all, the certainty that they can lead a comfortable old age. For them, being No. 1 for economic growth is meaningless unless it converts into a better life.

In this, the Japanese are no different from the Americans, or Europeans, or other Asians, or virtually any people in the world. They do not judge their economy solely, or even predominantly, by how dynamic or vigorous it is but by what it gives them. Only Japanese leaders, whose interests are served by the existing system, or foreigners, who enjoy believing that the Japanese are somehow unique, could possibly assume that producing more GNP is the be-all and end-all of economic endeavor.

When Is It Coming?

The first version of this book was entitled *Japan: The Coming Economic Crisis*. This time I have opted for (coming) as a sign that the crisis is already much closer. Indeed, in many ways, in many places, and for many people, the crisis has already arrived. But it is only the start and there is more to come. Those who read this book will be in a much better position to see the deterioration of the economy, as the "miracle" turns into a mirage.

Actually, the use of a word like "coming" is entirely justified. An economic crisis, unlike a personal or political crisis, is usually a gradual process. There is a bit of weakness, some partial failures, a touch of malaise at first. The weakness, failures and malaise then spread to afflict more of the economy. It is hard to say at exactly which point the crisis has struck. But its progression can be readily tracked.

What is faster than a speeding train? Japan's
super-economy. What else?

Credit: Foreign Press Center/Kyodo

For example, there is the relatively straightforward aspect
of economic growth. Annual growth of 4 or 5 percent is quite
handsome for some countries. And others would wish they
had as much. Nonetheless, it marks a definite slowdown for
an economy that had been racing ahead at 10 percent. Obviously, 5 percent is still growth, and even 1 percent implies
growth. But the lower the growth rate falls, the slower the
economy is expanding. And, if high economic growth only
improved living standards and financial security modestly, it
is possible that they could already deteriorate during periods
of sluggish growth. So, it would be foolish to wait for zero
growth before speaking of a crisis.

When an economy weakens, it does not do so all at once.
Certain sectors normally go before others. The usual sequence
is for farming and mining to suffer, followed by more labor-

intensive industries like textiles, garments and sundries. It takes longer for more advanced sectors to fail. And protected sectors can hold on for quite some time although they make little positive contribution. Services are rather varied, some disappearing early on, others surviving even the roughest times.

Similarly, geographic regions are not affected evenly. The rot usually starts in those areas that rely too heavily on the first sectors to weaken. That includes farming and fishing villages, towns that depend on coal or other mines, localities which lived off one or two factories in declining industries. Most of these areas are peripheral and it takes much longer before larger cities are affected, although they can be hurt, too. More immune to any economic crisis is the capital city, the center of commercial, financial and corporate activities, which is sustained by those operations and also helped by government spending.

For such reasons, the impact of a weakening economy differs from one segment of the population to another. Farmers, fishermen and miners are frequently hurt first, unless they obtain government handouts and subsidies or possess assets like land. Relatively uneducated and poorly trained workers, particularly those in declining industries, will probably lose their jobs soonest or have to accept low pay and long hours to subsist. But eventually even workers in more advanced sectors, technicians, white-collar employees and managers may be laid off. If not, they will doubtlessly be paid less and have trouble getting by.

When the economic weakness is evenly spread, all sectors, regions and population groups being hurt equally, it may be harder to detect. However, in most cases, there is a tendency for some to prosper even when others fall on hard times. Indeed, no matter how bad things get, it is possible for certain groups to accumulate great wealth. This results in a more visible polarization, with haves and have-nots, rich and poor.

Admittedly, today's crisis can be alleviated by shifting assets to today's requirements. Governments can spend their way out of a recession by engaging in more public works or reducing taxes. But they will be taking away resources that should be laid aside to meet tomorrow's needs. Nowadays, that means not having enough funds to cover the costs of a rapidly aging population. Thus, social security and welfare will suffer, slowing down the approach of the crisis but making it more acute when it finally arrives.

There is another way that an economic crisis can not only be put off but make present growth more impressive. That is by exporting more goods abroad, even if this brings in relatively little profit (or none at all). At least you are keeping your factories running, your workers on the job and your companies in business. Admittedly, some of your trading partners may be stuck with more closures, unemployment and bankruptcies due to such a "beggar thy neighbor" policy. But you can do all right as long as they do not react. Alas, they must react one day because they cannot bear trade and payments deficits forever.

To explain the situation in more general terms, this section was written without specific reference to Japan. Still, anyone familiar with the situation will know that each and every aspect applies. Over the decade since the original crisis book appeared, the economy has slowed down, certain sectors have weakened, villages, towns and even cities have slumped, more and more people are either needy or less comfortable than before, and too little has been done to ensure a better future.

The crisis has thus been spreading and deepening. For some, it is still coming. For others, it is already here. Another decade from now, certainly there will be many more who directly feel the crisis and even its surface manifestations should be visible to all who wish to see. Then I may produce a new edition which can drop the word "coming."

Ready Or Not . . .

Anyone who browses through the books-on-Japan section of a bookstore or library will immediately notice that there are many more focusing on Japan's economic prowess than a coming crisis. Indeed, some may feel that putting the word "crisis" in a book title is mere sensationalism. Such accusations were made when the original crisis book appeared and more should greet this updated version. Yet, there is no question but that the situation has worsened between the two publication dates, showing that a crisis book was more useful and justifiable than many of the prowess books.

In all fairness to those who deny that a crisis is coming, if not those who insist that a crisis is impossible in Japan, it must be conceded that this crisis was not so easy to detect initially.

As noted, economic growth is relative and Japan, while growing less rapidly than before, is still advancing at a fair clip. Even now, it is expanding faster than other advanced nations. Also, the slowdown was gradual. While some economic sectors, geographic regions and social categories have suffered, others are still doing reasonably well. Moreover, by skimping on social security and welfare and exporting come what may, it was possible to defer the worst effects.

Still, anyone with eyes to see must realize that some peripheral regions have been badly hit, certain industries have nearly been wiped out and life is harder for many people. It is generally known that, even among salaried employees in Tokyo, hours are long, commuting is painful and it is necessary to make do with inadequate housing and amenities. In addition to the worse-off, there are the outright poor who can be found sleeping on park benches or camping in subway stations. This means that those who reject the crisis thesis either do not see or do not bother looking.

One reason why many foreigners (and also Japanese) are unaware of the extent of the crisis is that they do not look in the right places. They dote on high tech sectors and forget declining ones. They insist that manufacturing, or at least parts of it, is doing nicely and overlook the mess in agriculture, mining, many services and distribution. They are familiar with big companies that pay higher wages and offer greater job security, but not the masses of smaller firms that do not. For them, the typical Japanese employee is the "salaryman," who happens to be part of an elite compared with blue-collar workers in general and those with smaller companies or temporary jobs in particular. Worse, they judge by what is going on in central Tokyo, where signs of prosperity abound, and not the more remote suburbs, let alone out-of-the-way mining, fishing and factory towns.

This is already bad enough. But many foreigners not only fail to see a crisis, they refuse to accept the very possibility of one arising. That may be because they have come to Japan in the expectation of finding an economic "miracle" and do not want to admit they were wrong. Or they do not know Japan well enough to even notice the telltale signs of crisis. These are, admittedly, not as noticeable as elsewhere because the Japanese like to put a good face on things, especially when dealing with foreigners. And many foreigners are too sensitive to pry.

There is also the matter of *tatemae* and *honne*, appearance and reality. The Japanese in general, and especially when dealing with outsiders (and foreigners are outsiders or *gaijin*), like to create an illusion of things being better than they actually are. Many foreigners fail to see through the *tatemae*. Many do not really want to know the *honne*.

But it is more than that. Journalists, who are paid to get

the facts, often come up with fiction. That is because they prefer a rousing good story, one that makes Japan look like a wonderland to the folks back home, and justifies the exorbitant cost of posting them to Tokyo. Thus, back in the 1960s, they wrote assiduously about the mammoth shipyards that built supertankers. Now that most of those are closed or building smaller boats, this is no longer a story. So they focus on biotechnology, or supercomputers, or some such.

When stories don't exist, they are invented. For example, the factories where "robots make robots." You must have read them. Well, in fact, robots only make parts but cannot assemble robots. So that idea is rather farfetched. I attended factory visits where Japanese managers admitted as much. But the journalists still went out and wrote florid pieces on futuristic factories, working around the clock, in which selfless and disciplined robots busily made robots like Santa's elves in the North Pole.

This was doubtlessly naive and perhaps mildly dishonest. But it pales compared to the articles and whole books that are written by professional Japanapologists, many of whom collect large sums of money for this activity one way or the other. They sometimes include journalists but more often foreign academics and think-tank publicists, supposed "scholars" who should be seeking the truth but are more than willing to accentuate the positive and eliminate the negative. They are rewarded, if not with cash, then with lecture fees, travel grants, scholarships, endowments, consulting contracts, book sales and so on.

The only imaginable advantage to this is that I still have more than enough silly quotes from eminent authorities to replace those in the last edition. These are actually even sillier because, over a decade ago, the situation was much better and it was easier to comprehend claims of a dynamic economy, satisfied workers, happy consumers and supportive public. Still, even today, there are sycophants who wax poetic about anything Japanese, from flower arrangement to welfare.

While many foreigners remain oblivious to the coming crisis, most Japanese are painfully aware of the problems. There is no shortage of criticism of the economy. Some of this comes from professional writers and the media, namely the major dailies and, more aggressively, the monthly and weekly magazines. Most Japanese academics, unlike their foreign counterparts, are also critical of Japanese-style economics and the social and political consequences. Indeed, there are more and more negative comments coming from establishment figures, leading politicians (not only in the opposition), retired career bureaucrats, top businessmen, even the prime minister on occasion.

As for the Japanese people, the supposed beneficiaries of the system, they have increasingly turned against it. The complaints are sometimes concrete, like excessive working hours and insufficient pay. But they also dislike the growing inequality and unfairness and are increasingly worried about the future. This can be gathered from private conversations with friends and colleagues (especially when inebriated) as well as formal public opinion polls, usually taken while the respondents were sober. The trends are fairly clear, steady . . . and negative.

Yet, the Japanese do not do much about it. There is a lot of griping and complaining among the people. There is some soul-searching and appeals for renewed efforts among the leaders. There are occasional official "reforms" and the odd "revolution." But nothing much changes. That has led some to assume that maybe the situation is not so bad. A safer hypothesis is that the Japanese do not know how to solve the problems or even have the gumption to tackle them.

Thus, the crisis should keep on coming. Only, it will do so in ways that remain undetected by most foreigners and many Japanese, especially those on the top. It will not take the form of an explosion, workers going out on strike, radicals burning down public buildings, ordinary folks boycotting political parties or refusing to buy the goods of offending companies. There will not be mass movements of disaffected employees, consumers, youths, women or the poor. Indeed, the ruling party may keep on ruling, company presidents may keep on giving orders, and bureaucrats may keep on meddling. But things will fall apart anyway.

The more likely scenario for Japan is implosion. After all, there are rather few legitimate forms of protest, the weak already know that they cannot accomplish as much by protesting as by selling their votes, the young have given up on trying to convince their elders and women on getting men to understand. Thus, while feigning suitable behavior in public, they go their own way in private.

This kind of crisis through implosion would be less visible because it is incremental and often hidden. But it would have much the same results. And, for the very reason that it is harder to detect, it would be harder to prevent and overcome.

2
Economic Miracles and Mirages

No More Growth Hero

Much of Japan's reputation as an economic "miracle" is based on its growth rate, once exceptionally—almost miraculously—high, now just quite ordinary. Thus, to understand why this reputation is no longer valid, it is helpful to take a big step back in time, to the late 1960s, when it was "discovered" by Herman Kahn. One of the first Japan-boosters, he was so sure of Japan's ability to grow at uncommonly fast rates that he went on record:

"It seems to me at least as likely as not that by 1975 the Japanese—and most of the outside world—will be expecting Japan to enjoy another twenty-five years of much the same growth rates. Or even if by 1975 the Japanese—or others—no longer expect Japan to match the greater than 10 percent per annum growth rates of the 1950–75 time period, they almost certainly will expect close to 10 percent and substantially more than the 'usual' 5 percent or so. . . . "[1]

It turned out that Herman Kahn was wrong. So were the Economic Planning Agency, various think tanks and assorted foreign "experts," all of whom expected Japan to remain a growth hero. For, far from achieving 10 percent growth, it actually averaged less than the "usual" 5 percent. This, one assumes, should have been enough to still the applause for Japan's economic prowess and undercut its reputation as a worker of "miracles." Apparently, it did not. On the very day I began writing this book, *Business Week* proclaimed, "after nearly five years of powerful growth, Japan's fleet-footed economy is showing its first real signs of fatigue."[2] Fleet-footed, indeed. This extraordinary growth was only just over 5 percent. Apparently, the "usual 5 percent" which once appeared so modest as to be beneath Japan was now quite an accomplishment.

And what if growth falls yet further? Will the many admirers be depressed. Probably not. The *Financial Times,* long a fan of the Japanese economy, announced: "growth is expected to slow to about 3 percent in 1992, lower than in recent years, but still impressive by most standards."[3] At this rate, if growth were to slip to 1 percent or even fall under zero, we can expect not only justifications but muted praise for having done so well. It seems that critics of the Japanese economy like myself will always be wrong as the standards are lowered.

We will thus have to contend with rather bizarre interpretations of the facts as well as the facts themselves. This is extremely important because, as stated, much of the case for Japan having a superior economy rests on its record for growth. It is supposedly stronger, more dynamic, more resilient than others. But this view can hardly be supported by even the most superficial reading of the past, which is obviously easier to forecast than the future and yet remains out of reach of much of the foreign media.

During the 1950s and 1960s, the Japanese economy did grow at an extraordinary rate of around 10 percent. During the 1970s, however, it only advanced by some 5 percent a year. And, in the 1980s, it was closer to 4 percent. This shows a dramatic deceleration of the economy, one which should be evident to any but the biased observer. Indeed, most articles and books should be dedicated, like this one, to explaining why the economy has been doing relatively poorly of late rather than inventing spurious explanations for an illusory success.

Admittedly, this cannot be seen in isolation. Japan's economic growth must be compared with performance elsewhere to see whether it maintained its edge. With regard to the West, this is done almost gleefully. The rest of the advanced nations also decelerated over the years. From about 4–5 percent during the 1950s and 1960s, they slowed down to some 2–3 percent. But this slowdown was not quite as sharp. And they never claimed to be growth heros anyway. They purposely sacrificed growth for other goals, including greater leisure, comfort and welfare. Whether they were right to do so will become clearer further on.

Still, if we are going to compare Japan to less dynamic economies, we can at least also compare it to more dynamic ones before speaking of growth that is "impressive by most standards." Let us therefore look East, to the newly industrialized countries (NICs) in its own backyard. For years, indeed, for decades Hong Kong, Korea, Singapore and Taiwan have been growing much more rapidly than Japan.[4]

The best that can be said for Japan is that it has managed to keep ahead of other advanced countries, although only by sacrificing other economic goals. Yet, it has fallen behind more vigorous economies quite dramatically. It is now in the middle of the pack, not leading it.

And that is only if you accept Japanese statistics at face value. As will be noted occasionally, Japanese statistics somehow differ from most other countries' statistics in significant ways. While nominal growth may be correct, *real* growth, which is what we are comparing, is not. It is obtained by using a deflator to adjust for inflation, and Japan's inflation figures can be very misleading. They are exceptionally low and certainly do not reflect increased housing, education and other costs adequately. If inflation were really higher, then growth would be lower. Enough so that Japan would not be faring that much better than many advanced countries and the "miracle" would be a "mirage."

So, let us consider the situation for inflation, another alleged achievement of this economy. Not only was it strong, the strength did not generate excessive inflation, almost a contradiction in terms elsewhere. Yet, going by the official statistics, over the past decade or so consumer price inflation was only about 3 percent a year and wholesale price inflation was half that (and often negative). Even Germany's inflation was slightly higher while it raced ahead at two, three and four times that rate in the United States, France and Italy.

Yet, as was intimated, inflation is very much a function of what the statisticians want it to be, for they are the ones who select the "basket" of goods against which it is measured. In Japan, there appears to be considerable underweighting of just those items whose prices rise faster while others, less variable over time, predominate. The most obvious culprit is land prices, which are admittedly an asset (and not counted) but also form part of housing costs, which should be heavily weighted. After all, housing is a substantial share of the family budget and the cost of land looms large in the cost of housing. Nonetheless, while consumer prices stagnated during the 1980s, land—and housing—prices soared as they had been doing ever since the 1950s. The same can be said of education costs, another big item.

That is perhaps why Japanese statisticians, as well as politicians, bureaucrats and businessmen make a distinction between rampant, almost runaway asset inflation, and moderate consumer price rises. Not surprisingly, this view is not shared by ordinary citizens who have to buy housing and find that mounting costs are squeezing out most other purchases. They know that the inflation figures are

Trends in Land and Consumer Price Indexes

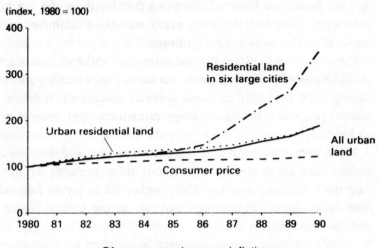

(index, 1980 = 100)

Of course, we have no inflation,
if you don't count land.

Source: Bank of Japan, *Economic Statistics*, 1991.
Credit: *Facts and Figures of Japan 1991*, p. 83.

meaningless and this should be borne in mind by foreigners as well if they want to evaluate the economy sensibly.

Another magnificent, if mythical achievement of the Japanese economy was to avoid unemployment, even in relatively hard times. The average rate remained well under 3 percent, while it was three and four times as high in the United States and Europe. Part of this was doubtlessly real. Rapid growth generates jobs, although less so in an economy obsessed with productivity and rationalization. Relative affluence draws workers into the services, which are more labor-intensive than manufacturing. And there is considerable flexibility in using labor.

One last explanation is less flattering, namely that the statisticians were again playing games. Indeed, they used so many artifacts that it would take pages to provide a thorough analysis.[5] In short, Japan did not count as jobless those who had been laid off, those who would be employed within a month, those who turned down a job offered by the labor exchange, those looking for work during the month but not the week of the survey, new entrants who had not yet worked, homeworkers and self-employed in general who had no work, etc. Moreover, many Japanese did not bother claiming to be unemployed for social or psychological reasons while others saw no point to it because unemployment compensation was so limited.

What with one thing and another, it is felt by many specialists that Japanese unemployment is appreciably higher than the official figure. The real level could easily be two or three times larger, depending on which factors are considered and the situation on the labor market. That would make Japan's performance just moderately better than that of other advanced countries. The only hope for a "solution" to the problem is that, over recent years, the birth rate has been steadily falling which means that there will be fewer and fewer new entrants who seek jobs in the future.

Unsteady As She Goes

Having disproved the myth that Japan's economy moved inexorably onward and upward, it is necessary to turn to a derivative, namely that it was progressing smoothly. This was supposedly an economy that was so well managed and so insulated from ordinary troubles that it could carry on come what may. Quite to the contrary, a close look at Japan's growth trajectory will show that it was very uneven. Growth could accelerate and decelerate quite radically, and quite suddenly, leaving businessmen and consumers very uncertain of the situation. Periodically, and certainly more often than they liked, it was also afflicted by what the Japanese call shocks or *shokku*.

One of the latest variations on the theme of steady-as-she-goes was an odd comment by the *Wall Street Journal* to the effect that "Japan has had only one recession since 1945."[6] That must have come as a big surprise to Japanese economists who regularly refer to the recessions of 1954 and 1965 along with the major one in 1973–75. This idea of a smooth ride is further belied by abrupt upticks deriving not from Japanese ingenuity but fortuity, namely the outbreak of the Korean and Vietnam wars which, while horrible misfortunes for others, stimulated the economy quite strongly.[7]

More recently, the downticks have predominated. One of the earliest, back in 1971, was caused by the "Nixon shock" when Washington imposed a surcharge on imports and suspended the dollar's convertibility. This hit Japan worst because it was so dependent on exports to the United States and sold more by keeping the yen artificially cheap. But this was just the beginning of an unending trade war, which spread from country to country. Soon the Europeans and Asians were equally upset by massive Japanese imports and inexplicable difficulties in selling to Japan. In retaliation, they restricted imports of one product after another, from textiles, to steel, to automobiles.[8]

This only worsened the situation for certain sectors which were relatively labor-intensive and became increasingly uncompetitive as Japan's own labor costs rose. In order to keep prices down, many companies opened factories abroad, either in cheaper Asian countries or in export markets to get around trade restrictions. The amount of investment increased rapidly, especially whenever the yen appreciated. By the 1970s, Japanese businessmen were complaining of a "hollowing" (*kudoka*) of the economy and the "doughnut phenomenon," where manufacturing was done abroad rather than at home.

By then, Japan was faced by rising imports from more backward economies which had a competitive edge for labor. This undermined some of its older industries, textiles, garments and simple electronics, first, then even steel and shipbuilding. This was just part of the growing list of declining or ailing sectors. More would be added after the two oil crises, since now certain raw materials were also more expensive, most notably oil needed to fuel many industries but also as feedstock for the petrochemical plants.

The first oil shock in 1973 had a dramatic impact. It threw Japan into its biggest postwar recession. Companies reacted quickly, reducing the oil content of production, switching to cheaper fuels and moving into new sectors. But the crisis was hardly "overcome," as was commonly claimed, it inflicted serious damage on many sectors. The second oil crisis, in 1979, was less punishing although it further undermined sectors dependent on oil. Worse, there was now less room to conserve oil in industry and private consumption only increased with the years.

In the mid-1980s, Japan underwent the *endaka* or "heavy yen" crisis. After keeping the yen artificially cheap for years, it was finally raised to a more reasonable level that would hopefully balance trade with the United States. This faint hope was shattered, since American exports did not increase commensurately and Washington assumed that imports were being blocked artificially. That led to yet more trade conflicts. Meanwhile, Japanese exports were hampered by higher prices. To reduce them, among other things, automation was augmented, workers were laid off, and yet more parts and products were manufactured abroad. This, of course, only exacerbated the hollowing.

The heavy yen, massive public works and loose monetary policy, part of this designed to boost domestic consumption and facilitate absorption of imports, had an unexpected effect. Enormous amounts of money flowed into land and financial instruments. Those who owned land, managed real estate, or held stocks made extraordinary profits. Some of this was saved but much more was spent. Indeed, Japan's once frugal population was soon engaged in an unseemly buying spree, using their own money or increasingly popular credit cards. Naturally, this stimulated consumption and made domestic demand a major source of growth. The result was the Heisei boom of the late 1980s, much praised in the foreign press.

In Japan, this period was more often referred to by the less flattering name of the "bubble economy." Even while the bubbles existed, the benefit of the boom was uncertain. After all, the big winners were only a small share of the population, and losers included everyone who had to buy or rent land and real estate. Then, when they burst, the bubbles had an unquestionably negative effect. They reduced the asset base of companies, banks and individuals, making them "poorer" again. Being poorer, they naturally consumed less and companies which had eagerly expanded production were stuck with excess capacity. Meanwhile, those who had unwisely speculated in land or stocks were in even worse shape. By the early 1990s, the number and value of bankruptcies was climbing rapidly.

Thus, while foreign admirers were crowing that Japan had finally "proved" it could grow through domestic demand rather than exports, that people were finally becoming truly affluent and that the economy was still vigorous, many Japanese angrily criticized the situation. Even the staid *Nihon Keizai Shimbun* (*Japan Economic Journal*) struck a wrathful tone:

"Behind the steady progress of structural transformation, the economy, awash with liquidity and carried away by boom psychology, came to take on other, unsavory aspects, such as rampant money games and land speculation. Economic growth is now under the parallel influences of a moderate slowdown in the real economy and the shock waves from burst speculative bubbles."[9]

This brings us back to the question of growth. Surely, any economy can grow when money is printed and spent wildly. But, even in Japan, such a binge must end and the time come for sobering up. That means that part of the longest postwar boom was definitely spurious. Some of the faster-than-usual growth of the late 1980s will result in slower-than-otherwise-necessary growth in the early 1990s. Alas, as we shall soon see, that is only one of the drawbacks of this kind of economic "progress."

What Went Wrong?

Why has the Japanese economy slowed down and growth become unsteady and sometimes unreal? Oddly enough, one of the more complete listings of negative factors was provided by Herman Kahn in *The Emerging Japanese Superstate*. Only, rather than take them seriously, he wrote them off as not being likely to have substantial impact in the near future. They were: drying up of imported technology, decreased growth and aging of the labor force, urge for more infrastructure and welfare, heavier defense expenditures, trouble over foreign trade, weakening work ethic and less interest in growth, rebellion of young people against accepted values, political strains, managerial sloppiness and an end to the feeling of being "one big family."[10]

As it turned out, all of these factors—and many more— were a drag on economic growth and will continue undermining the economy for decades to come. It is hard to grasp why Kahn and other Japanapologists did not realize that long ago. It was already painfully clear to many Japanese economists, writers and ordinary citizens as well as more realistic foreigners, who were naturally branded pessimists and Japanbashers. Most of these factors were mentioned in the first edition of this book and several more have been added to this edition. Although they will be considered in greater detail further on, it does not hurt to provide a brief description of the changing economic environment here.

Japan's extraordinary growth during the 1950s and 1960s

can be explained by many things. The Japanese and their boosters quite rightly stress hard work, spirit of sacrifice, willingness to cooperate, ingenuity, attention to quality, pro-growth policies, and so on. But there were certain other elements which must also be considered yet rarely are. They do not so much detract from Japan's achievements as explain why they were possible.

First of all, and this refers to all statistics, it is always easier to show impressive growth when you begin near the bottom. Japan's index of industrial and other production was exceedingly low after defeat in the war and devastation of the economy. It was not surprising that, starting from such a base, the movement should be slanted upward.

This movement could be that much faster during the initial period when the task was more to restore than create. The first steps did not involve introducing new industries, training unskilled workers and building more factories. Rather, highly skilled workers were shifted from wartime to peacetime pro-duction. They already had the knowhow and experience and companies were, for the most part, producing articles that were familiar or similar. Steelmakers just made more steel. Automakers made trucks instead of tanks. That was hard. But not so hard. And the same thing was being done all over Europe.

Of course, if Japan had not been allowed to concentrate on economic recovery, the process would have been pains-takingly slow. In this case, the occupying power actually promoted economic development. General MacArthur's staff did what it could to revive industry so goods could be pro-duced locally and workers and ex-soldiers could find jobs. In many ways, they helped Japan obtain capital, technologies and markets. They even brought in the first productivity ex-perts. And, lest it be forgotten, they put down the leftist parties and trade unions and allowed management to regain control over their employees.

Unlike Germany, Japan was let off easy. It only paid some minor, token reparations before those ceased and Japan could use whatever funds were generated for its own growth. In addition, although rarely mentioned nowadays, the economy benefited from massive financial assistance. While not as structured as the Marshall Plan, the United States did supply significant aid, estimated at something like $2 billion up to 1951.[11] In those days, that was a lot of money. Japan also received loans from the World Bank and other international bodies.

Meanwhile, once again unlike the Europeans, Japan was able to enjoy the Pax Americana without participating. The Pacific was no less a scene of cold war tensions than Europe and Japan's next-door neighbors were China, North Korea and Russia, all of them armed to the teeth and aggressive. Yet, it was only expected to support a small, rather tame military and counted for its true defense on the American nuclear umbrella. Japan's defense budget throughout the postwar period revolved around 1 percent of gross domestic product, a truly modest cost for such effective deterrence.

This is another point the Japanese, and their supporters, repeatedly gloss over. For them, it was only a minor contribution to economic growth, if that. Such a conclusion is hard to comprehend. Year after year, for five decades, the Japanese spent 2–3 percent less GDP than Europeans and 4–5 percent less than Americans on defense. This was not millions or even billions of dollars, it amounted to trillions. And all that money could be poured into alternative uses, industrial production being foremost.

The new world order, erected and maintained by the Americans with little help from the Japanese, created a congenial context for growth in other ways. Most significant was the constant expansion of trade. This was extremely important for Japan because it had again adopted an export-oriented approach similar to the prewar period. It concentrated on industries which could produce large quantities of consumer goods, quantities so large that they could only be absorbed by exports. And export they did. Companies opened one market after the other, most readily in the United States, then Southeast Asia, Europe, even the Communist bloc. Export growth was amazingly swift and it pulled along the rest of the economy.

It was even more satisfactory when another aspect is considered. Trade expansion was greatly facilitated by the reduction of trade barriers. By far the biggest beneficiary was Japan. If it had also been a major contributor, then this would have been fair enough. Instead, in one round after the other, the Japanese got considerably more than they gave. They held on to their tariffs and quotas, their nontariff barriers and control of distribution channels, much longer than others. Certainly, this one-sided approach helped exports while impeding imports.

During the whole period, Japanese companies upgraded their technologies. They deserve enormous credit for their effort. But it would never have borne fruit so rapidly if not for the fact that they could readily acquire foreign knowhow. That saved lots of time on trial and error and invention. From the start, the Japanese had proven technologies to make products for which there already existed markets. All that remained was to make the products somewhat cheaper, or somewhat better, or both, than competitors.

This catching up process was amazingly cheap. In fact, initially foreign companies vied with one another to sell technology to the Japanese. According to one authority, Japan's total payments for imported technology from 1952–80 amounted to $45–50 billion. That was less than the United States spent on R&D in 1980 alone. For that price, Japan "got basically the whole stock of the new technology created by foreign countries." It was, indeed, "the greatest fire sale in history."[12]

By the 1970s, this situation was changing. Either the positive aspects were less significant or they had been used up. That was partly a concomitant of maturity. It also derived from a belated realization by its benefactor, America, that it had been too lenient and was taken advantage of. Most other countries were less willing to cooperate on Japan's terms.

Thus, trade expansion was slackening. Trade was still growing worldwide, but at a slower pace. And there was more competition than ever for the same markets since more countries had become export-oriented. Those which had not, and experienced substantial worsening of their trade balance, became more defensive and protective. New trade barriers were erected in the United States, Europe and Third World, although they were sometimes called restraint or orderly marketing agreements. Japan, which had become used to entering one market after the other, found there were few new ones left and older ones were harder to penetrate.

As Japanese companies rose along the learning curve, it became ever harder to acquire new technologies. There were not as many sophisticated ones which had not yet been used and by now the owners were less willing to sell or, if they did, demanded much higher prices. This meant that companies had to engage in their own research and development, a more costly and time-consuming process than buying or borrowing and then adapting or improving existing technologies. Worse, you never knew whether the R&D effort would generate enough new products to justify the increasingly heavy expenditures.

Finally, Japan was now expected to carry more of the defense and aid burden. Luckily for it, with *glasnost* and *perestroika,* it no longer had to worry about its neighbors and could still keep its defense budget small. But, as a rich, advanced country, it was supposed to contribute more and more to poorer, less developed countries. Gradually, its development aid grew, making the largest contribution overall but still far from generous in per capita terms. When taken all together, defense, aid and diplomacy, Japan merely enjoyed a fairly cheap, but not quite free, ride.[13]

Excuses, Excuses

Eventually, even the staunchest champions of the Japanese "miracle" noticed that growth was slowing down and the economy was becoming less vigorous. When they cast about for reasons, more often than not they sought them less in what Japan was doing wrong than what others were doing to it. This slowdown, these setbacks, they were somehow the fault of others. Four of the more widespread apologies are dealt with here, but there are many more.

For years after the oil crisis, this horrible *shokku* was blamed for most of Japan's ills despite the fact that, in almost the same breath, admirers argued that Japan had done a superlative job of "overcoming" the crisis. Yet, Japan was hardly alone. Every industrialized country faced the same difficulties and most of them were as dependent on imported oil. Yet, according to the statistics, Japan's manufacturing output fell more than the OECD average. And its growth dropped from over 10 percent to around 5 percent, an awesome loss of five percentage points, far worse than occurred in the West. Yes, Japan did scrape through, but certainly no better than others.

Admittedly, the oil crises of 1973 and 1979 were external events, unleashed from without, and Japan could not be held responsible for them. But it should have known that they could occur, assuming it was really an information society, and it could have prepared. Instead, it was among the last to realize there was trouble in the Middle East. And it had foolishly targeted all sorts of industries that were heavily dependent on oil and energy (petrochemicals, light metals, production of oil tankers, etc.). No wonder it got hurt worse.

Anyway, the first oil crisis was about two decades ago. If

the high cost of oil can be blamed for undercutting growth then, why is it that growth did not accelerate when oil became comparatively cheap? Perhaps because, among other things, the economy was already slowing down *before* the oil crisis. More ominous for the future, one reason Japan reacted as well as it did was that in the early 1970s industry was the main consumer of oil. It moved quickly to reduce consumption by using more efficient techniques. Now oil and energy consumption are expanding rapidly, wiping out the former gains, because the population is using more than ever. That will make any future oil shock more painful.

The heavy yen (*endaka*) crises have also been blamed on foreigners, this time the Americans. Superficially, this can be justified by Nixon's decision in 1971 and the Plaza Accord of 1985. But it is naive to assume that they would have had any effect if the yen were not substantially undervalued (usually as a result of government policy to keep the yen cheap and promote exports). For, otherwise, the yen would have sunk again. It takes no genius to realize that if Japan regularly exports more than it imports, its currency will rise while those of deficit countries fall. This is a normal occurrence.

Japanese views on the trade imbalance have taken an even uglier, more personal turn. Increasingly, any trouble is traced not to objective events but subjective reactions that are attributed to envy or ill will. Americans and Europeans are jealous of Japan for selling so much. They cannot produce quality goods and are angry that Japan defeats them in fair competition. This may even be tinged with racism and revanchism. That this is no exaggeration can be gathered from the comments of Osamu Shimomura, a former Bank of Japan official, who wrote in the aptly titled bestseller ''Japan Is Not At Fault, America Is:''

''The United States cannot bear to be the loser, and so it concludes that free trade means arranging things so it cannot

lose. Doubtless this attitude reflects the belief in excellence—
its own excellence. America believes that by rights it ought
to be stronger than Japan; since it cannot be, it tries to hold
Japan back."[14]

These Japanese views are obviously as subjective as similar
foreign ones and thus easy to discard for objective reasons.
Even if one accepts the idea that American industry is inefficient, American products are shoddy, and American workers
are lazy, that would only explain why the United States runs
a perennial deficit. It does not explain the case of Europe, in
particular a pretty competitive Germany. Nor can it possibly
justify the difficulty of the East Asian NICs. Korea, Taiwan
and Hong Kong are all extremely productive and, in addition,
cheap. Their exports have repeatedly defeated the Japanese
competition on third markets. Yet, they cannot sell these same
goods in Japan.

What is most inexplicable here is that Japan seems to be
competitive across the whole spectrum. That it can compete
against capital and technology-intensive products from advanced countries, which have similar factor endowments, is
comprehensible. But it cannot also be competitive for labor-
intensive goods against countries whose labor costs are a fifth
or a tenth as high. Not if there is any such thing as comparative
advantage. For Japan to win all around, there must be other
causes which would inevitably include trade barriers and inter-company links.

But nothing the Japanese said was quite as cockeyed as
what its foreign friends contended. The *Financial Times,* in
a forceful editorial, not only excused Japan's enormous—and
increasingly worrisome—trade surplus but deemed it absolutely positive. For Japan could invest this money in other
countries. "The world economy needs Japan's current account surplus to resume its rising trend," the editorialist insisted.[15] It never occured to him that, had trade been more

balanced, those countries could have kept the money and invested locally, in local companies, to boost the local economy, without going into debt with Japan.

When not proffering excuses, the apologists adopt another tack. They claim that Japan's failures are not "failures" at all. What happened was not only desired but actively sought and brought about by the Japanese. This was simply further proof that the economy was superbly managed.

For example, Japan was not afflicted with the same ailment as other advanced countries of aging and declining sectors. To the contrary, it was purposely shedding industries in which it was either no longer competitive or did not wish to compete. The former were the "throw-away industries" and the latter remnants of "early-stage industrialization," according to correspondents of *The Economist.*[16] The first group included coal, non-ferrous metals, paper pulp and agricultural produce, the second, cotton textiles, sewing machines, pottery, etc. True, Japan did not make much fuss about the fate of bicycles or pottery, but for every other product bureaucrats came up with ingenious plans to support them and prolong their existence. No major industry was allowed to succumb if it could be saved by subsidies, protection and cartels. But that did not keep guru Peter Drucker from proclaiming that Japan's business leaders and bureaucrats were increasingly convinced that "manufacturing work does not belong in a developed country such as Japan."[17]

As noted, the recent shift from export-led growth to one sustained more by domestic demand was supposedly managed by the government. That it was not has already been explained. But a word might be added to the effect that it cannot. During the 1950s and 1960s, when companies were still weak and dependent on government finance and protection, businessmen did listen to bureaucrats and often complied with their wishes. Now that companies are strong and self-reliant, and businessmen know what they want, they either go their own way or subject bureaucrats to their whims. There will be no shift until this is decided by corporate leaders and that is not even part of their agenda.

Still, the belief in bureaucratic omnipotence survives. During the worldwide stock market crash of 1987, Tokyo's market slipped much less than others. That was, we were told, due to cooperation between the public and private sectors. Perhaps it was. But, if they were so mighty, why did the Tokyo market collapse in 1991 when most others were doing fairly well? A failure by the bureaucrats? No. Most assuredly not. This was a deliberate action not only to cool off but revamp the economy.

"The party was brought to an end deliberately, by the Bank of Japan. It raised interest rates five times from mid-1989 to mid-1990, in the hope of squeezing the speculative bubbles in the stock and property markets before they burst on their own. . . . Those were the central bank's explicit aims. But it also had implicit ones. In effect, its tight-money policy is intended to bring about a shift in the domestic economy . . . out of low-tech, inefficient manufacturing and cartelised, inefficient services, such as wholesale and retail distribution."[18]

Chalk another one up for Japan, Inc. It always does the right thing at the right time. That the American Fed and German Bundesbank adopted exactly the same posture does not win them any respect or show that Japan was not so special. Nor does one bother mentioning that the Japanese economy had exaggerated more than others and that these measures therefore hurt companies worse. Nor, indeed, was anything said when the Bank of Japan suddenly relaxed policy, well before it had a chance to work fully.

As for the economy's "hollowing," that was supposedly caused by a mixture of foresight and magnanimity. On the one hand, Japanese companies realized well in advance that they were no longer competitive for certain articles and moved production abroad. On the other, they invested for the good of the countries involved, to strengthen their technologies and upgrade their economies. The latter comment hardly needs to be refuted, since most investments were clearly made for reasons of profit and not charity. The former is also grossly misleading. While more enlightened companies like Sony and Honda invested early on, most others came much later. And they were often panicked into it by currency revaluation or trade barriers.[19] Anyway, whatever the cause, the "doughnut" phenomenon could not be avoided although Japan tried its best.

From this brief tour of fantasyland, two things must be obvious. One is that no proposition is too preposterous and no apology too audacious for the faithful friends of Japan. Trust and logic be damned, when Japan is criticized they leap to its defense with whatever argument sounds good at the time (no matter now silly it appears when properly analyzed). The other is that, if we are ever to understand the workings and accomplishments of the Japanese economy, we must discard these excuses, apologies and red herrings and take a much closer look at the real situation.

NOTES

1. Herman Kahn, *The Emerging Japanese Superstate*, p. 2.
2. *Business Week*, September 16, 1991, p. 47.
3. *Financial Times*, September 11, 1991, p. 12.
4. See Jon Woronoff, *Asia's "Miracle" Economies*.
5. See Koji Taira, "Japan's Low Unemployment: Economic Miracle or Statistical Artifact?", *Monthly Labor Review*, July 1983, pp. 3–10. See also Jon Woronoff, *Japan's Wasted Workers*, pp. 224–61.
6. *Wall Street Journal*, January 24, 1991, A7.
7. For more about Japan's economic rise, see Yutaka Kosai, *The Era of High-Speed Growth*, Takafusa Nakamura, *The Postwar Japanese Economy*, Myohei Shinohara, *Industrial Growth, Trade and Dynamic Pat-*

terns in the Japanese Economy, and Tatsuro Uchino, *Japan's Postwar Economy.*

8. See Edward J. Lincoln, *Japan's Unequal Trade,* and Woronoff, *World Trade War.*
9. *Nikkei Weekly,* September 7, 1991.
10. Kahn, op. cit., pp. 104–6.
11. See Uchino, op. cit., pp. 262–3.
12. Ronald Dore, *Japan Economic Survey,* May 1986, p. 6.
13. For more on the future difficulties, see Lincoln, *Facing Economic Maturity.*
14. Osamu Shimomura, *Nippon wa warukunai: warui no wa America da,* Tokyo, Bungei Shinju, 1987, quoted in Kenneth B. Pyle, "The Burden of Japanese History," in John H. Makin (ed.), *Sharing World Leadership?,* Washington, American Enterprise Institute, 1989.
15. *Financial Times,* January 24, 1992, p. 12.
16. Correspondents of The Economist, *Consider Japan,* London, Duckworth, 1963.
17. Peter F. Drucker, "Japan: New Strategies for a New Reality," *Wall Street Journal,* October 2, 1991.
18. *The Economist,* April 27, 1991, p. 35.
19. See Woronoff, *Japan's Commercial Empire.*

3

Economic Super-Management

Planning And Targeting, Sort Of

Another of the arguments for Japan's economy being different—and superior—is rooted in the idea that it was managed more expertly than others. It was also, in the view of many supporters, managed more dynamically and effectively by astute bureaucrats who adopted a hands-on approach. They supposedly decided in which directions the economy should move and then got it there, if possible by coaxing and cajoling businessmen, if necessary by giving instructions and orders through actual legislation or more subtle administrative guidance (*gyosei shido*).

These bureaucrats occupied key posts in the Ministry of International Trade and Industry (MITI), Ministry of Finance (MOF) and Economic Planning Agency (EPA), among other bodies. They were quite extraordinary beings in the view of foreign bureaucratophiles, although few Japanese businessmen or ordinary citizens thought as highly. According to Chalmers Johnson, they constituted "a powerful, talented and prestige-laden bureaucracy."[1] In the view of Norman Macrae of *The Economist*, they were the "most mathematically-minded on earth."[2] And what they wrought has filled many a book on the Japanese economic "miracle."

Initially, the primary focus was on Japanese planning, which seemed incredibly successful back in the 1960s when planning and *dirigisme* were fashionable. One exceptionally enthusiastic fan was Norman Macrae, who called the Japanese economy the "most intelligently *dirigiste* system in the world today." According to him, "the ultimate responsibility for industrial planning, for deciding in which directions Japan's burgeoning effort should try to go, and for fostering and protecting business as it moves in those directions, lies with the government."[3]

Considering Japan's dynamic economic growth, one can understand why planning looked good then. However, scrutinizing the planning apparatus itself, one should already have had some doubts at the time. For the bureaucrats inhabiting the Economic Planning Agency were not economists, let alone planners, but quite ordinary pen-pushers. Worse, in Japan's hierarchical administration, they only represented an agency and not a ministry, and one that was of very recent origin. So, they could not obtain much cooperation from other bureaucracies, each of which initiated its own plans and managed its own budgets. Nor could they impose on companies since they had no control over their activities.

Consequently, the plans were indicative, and very clearly marked so. They began with high-sounding preambles about Japan's will and ability to grow but provided few specifics. In practice, if other bureaucrats or businessmen did what the plan foresaw, it was because they also felt it was the appropriate action to take in their own interest. This tended to occur more in the 1950s and 1960s, when the recovery was still frail and businessmen less sure of their own capabilities. By the 1970s, however, plans were little more than declarations of intention or PR sheets.

By the 1980s, when planning was less fashionable and free enterprise more warmly endorsed, Prime Minister Nakasone discarded the notion of genuine planning as inappropriate.

Still, while you could scrap planning, you could not dismiss the bureaucrats, so they continued turning out "plans" of a sort. For the Nakasone era, this was reduced to a compilation of "prospects and guidelines for the 1980s." Later on, it was just a question of "master plans" full of good sentiments and little else, such as the one for 1988–92 entitled "A Japan That Cohabits With The World." As per usual, one plan was often replaced by another even before its time had come, simply because each new prime minister liked to put his name on a plan no matter how trivial.[4]

This must be mentioned before evaluating the "results" of planning. For they can be very misleading. During the early plans of the 1950s and 1960s, the technique seemed to be working as growth rates powered ahead by 10 percent and more, usually outstripping already ambitious targets. By the 1970s, however, growth rates regularly came in well beneath the official targets. While the former was doubtlessly more agreeable, both overfulfilling and underfulfilling plans by wide margins showed that there was little connection between the plans and what actually happened. This was only avoided by recent plans through the expedient of not having numerical objectives.

The passing of planning was hardly lamented (except by EPA bureaucrats), for now foreign observers had discovered an even more extraordinary expression of Japan's superior economic management. It became known as industrial policy or "targeting," for short. This time the Ministry of International Trade and Industry was in charge, the most formidable body yet conceived according to some. These bureaucrats carefully examined the various industries Japan could enter and picked the right ones, then shifted resources massively toward companies which could thrive in those areas, and helped them become world-class competitors.

The MITIocrats did this by studying not only Japan's present but also its future comparative advantage so that it could

Planning is easy. Only the implementation is hard.

Name of Plan	Dates Initiator	Growth Target (Actual Growth)
Five Year Plan For Economic Self-Reliance	1956–1960 Hatoyama	4.9% (8.8%)
New Long-Term Economic Plan	1958–1962 Kishi	6.5% (9.7%)
National Income Doubling Plan	1961–1970 Ikeda	7.8% (10.0%)
Mid-Term Economic Plan	1964–1968 Sato	8.1% (10.1%)
Economic And Social Development Plan	1967–1971 Sato	8.2% (9.8%)
New Economic And Social Development Plan	1970–1975 Sato	10.6% (5.1%)
Economic And Social Basic Plan	1973–1977 Tanaka	9.4% (3.5%)
Economic Plan 1976–80	1976–1980 Miki	6.0% (4.5%)
New Seven-Year Economic And Social Plan	1979–1985 Ohira	5.7% (3.9%)

get into the right sectors earlier and develop more quickly than was normally feasible. To help the process along, the government provided financial assistance, protection against imports, special R&D programs and whatever else was needed. Businessmen went along because either they respected MITI's ability (the less probable alternative) or they were eager for funds and support (the more likely conclusion).[5]

Targeting was obviously a more "real" exercise than planning because MITI did command considerable resources. It was also more successful, since bureaucrats often picked suitable targets. By using those resources, they were able to get companies into the right sectors earlier than otherwise and help them grow faster than would ordinarily occur. They did not always "pick winners," but they managed to get more targets right than wrong. That was no mean achievement. Success stories included textiles, steel, electronics, computers, semiconductors and many more. Others ministries or agencies undertook similar programs, the Ministry of Transport for shipbuilding, Ministry of Post and Telecommunications for telecom equipment, and so on.

But this is still no reason to overlook the failures. First of all, MITI missed out on some sectors, like motorcycles, automobiles and biotechnology until late in the day. It failed to come through for aerospace. Worse, it backed some losers as well, namely light metals and petrochemicals. In addition, when targeting was exaggerated, the outcome was excess capacity which hurt the sector, as in the case of shipbuilding, shipping, light metals and perhaps even steel. Equally disconcerting is the fact that by the 1970s the bureaucrats were as busy rescuing ailing sectors as promoting futuristic ones like advanced computers and satellites.

In conceding targeting's general success, it should not be overlooked that many other sectors managed to develop pretty much on their own, including consumer electronics and automobiles. Companies which refused to cooperate also did quite nicely, including pioneers like Honda, Sony and Kyocera, all of which had some grief with the bureaucracy. Moreover, the companies participating in targeting exercises were usually major ones, while smaller companies had to get along on their own.

By now, targeting has also been phased out to some extent, although there are still substantial ongoing projects and collusion between bureaucrats and businessmen is almost second nature. However, since foreign countries have finally realized that industrial policy worked, largely to their detriment, the government is just as happy to keep it quiet. This was also done because fashions have changed once again and government intervention is no longer popular. This could be noted from more recent comments by that trendsetter Norman Macrae, who subsequently claimed that Japan succeeded because it had the "lowest level of government interference." As for his earlier enthusiastic remarks, they were "always balderdash."[6]

Financial Wizardry

Japan also enjoys an enviable reputation, in the West at least, for the way its financial policy is run. Once again, it was left largely to bureaucrats rather than politicians, as in most other democratic nations. This would have been a cause for concern, or so it seems, if not for the extraordinary reputation of the financial bureaucrats. Those in the Ministry of Finance were long regarded as the "elite of the elite," probably because they graduated from the most elite universities. But it would be difficult to find any hard evidence of this in what they did.

In one particular, they do appear to have performed admirably and contributed mightily to Japan's rapid economic growth. That was by channeling vast amounts of money, at very cheap rates, to the major companies which were often included in MITI's targeting exercises as well as others which rebuilt industry. Numerous studies have shown that these companies obtained funds at extremely low costs, first through the banks, then by issuing stock on a bouyant market.

However, while cheap rates helped companies, it hurt individual savers who received lower rates. In fact, there were times when ordinary savings accounts earned negative returns because interest rates were lower than inflation. Even in the best of times, gains were exceedingly modest. This means that the Japanese people were subsidizing Japanese companies whether they wished to or not. For they were given no choice. All banks offered the same rates and it was not easy to send money abroad. Only in the 1980s, under pressure from foreign countries rather than the populace, was the financial sector deregulated so that ordinary Japanese could get a decent return.

The Ministry of Finance and Bank of Japan were also credited, again more by foreigners than natives, with running such smooth monetary policies that they avoided many unnecessary ups and downs. Yet, as we saw, there were occasional recessions as well as sudden upturns in the economy. And they could often be traced to periods of excessive monetary tightness or looseness. This is what is usually known as "stop-and-go" in other countries so it must be assumed that the financial bureaucrats overshot in both directions as well. When their aim apparently went wild was the late 1980s.

As noted earlier, there was an impressive expansion from 1986–91, partly fueled by monetary laxity and heavy public works spending. Some of this was due to foreign pressure, the rest derived from bureaucratic efforts to help business by keeping money cheap. Alas, much of this cheap money did not go into productive investment or better amenities but land, stock, art and other financial assets. These were some of the bubbles in a "bubble economy" which, while paralleled by similar phenomena abroad, was considerably more bloated and grotesque in Japan.

This was hardly a period the bureaucrats could be proud of, despite the economic growth. It allowed companies to engage in money games through financial management (*zaiteku*) rather than concentrate on business. It permitted speculators to accumulate enormous wealth through land and stock transactions. Few ordinary citizens benefited to any great extent through stocks and, for those whose land increased in value, this was usually a paper gain because they could not sell. Not only had the bureaucrats let prices get out of hand, they were responsible for overlooking questionable or outright dishonest practices by those they were supposed to supervise, including banks and securities houses.

Moreover, like all bubbles, these had to burst one day, even though collusion between bureaucrats and businessmen or among businessmen delayed the process. Still, by the early 1990s, land prices were sinking enough to worry the authorities, if not quite enough to offer much relief to home buyers. Then, despite government efforts to prop up the stock market, the index began declining and ended in a free fall. The Nikkei average lost nearly 60 percent of its value at the lowest point, one of the worst crashes in world history. Alas, the losers were not so much the speculators as ordinary individuals who were trapped in investment funds or whose money was poorly invested by insurance and pension managers.

This revealed that the "longest postwar expansion" in the 1980s was partly spurious. Companies had built more capacity than was needed, investors had put money into sectors that were already bloated, and the boom was bound to give way to a bust. This economic downturn was already unpleasant but it was further aggravated by the discovery of countless scandals in banks, securities and real estate firms as well as among the politicians and bureaucrats. As for the Ministry of Finance, its officials hardly behaved like the "elite of the elite" and were largely to blame for the abuses. This almost caused a loss of authority, but the bureaucrats fought hard to retain their prerogatives and won.

The record was also dubious with regard to another aspect of financial management, namely fiscal policy. For years, the Ministry of Finance enjoyed a solid reputation for keeping the government within budget. Indeed, it even managed to expand the budget regularly without incurring deficits. That, however, was much easier during the 1950s and 1960s, when the economy was growing rapidly and revenue rose automatically without having to raise taxes. Once the economy slowed, and Japan's bureaucrats faced the same sort of problems as in other countries, they performed considerably less well. During the 1970s, Japan regularly ran a deficit, a deficit of as much as 30 percent or much higher than the United States or Europe.[7]

This deficit, which continued into the 1980s, was clearly getting out of hand. The total mount of debt spiraled ever higher and reached a cumulative ¥170 trillion by the early 1990s. At that time, Tokyo was doing worse than supposedly more profligate places like Washington and London. Distressingly, the bureaucrats did not seem capable of stopping the hemorrhage. And the politicians did not want it stopped, since they enjoyed launching new public works and other projects. Ultimately, with its reputation at stake, the Ministry of Finance managed to cut back on the issue of new bonds and, helped by the boom of the late 1980s, the share of new debt was reduced (although the total debt was not).

But so many bonds had been issued by then that debt servicing was a steadily growing share of the budget. By 1991, 23 percent of the general account budget was earmarked for paying off the debt rather than providing goods and services of use to the public. Moreover, even this success was questionable when you consider that off-budget expenditures had never ceased mounting. The Fiscal Investment and Loan Program (FILP) was spending huge amounts equal to as much as 40 percent of the ordinary budget, year after year. Since this money was invested in public works and state corporations, it was actually a responsibility of the government. And since few of these projects earned a decent return, and many lost huge amounts (like the railways), the government might eventually have to ante up.

To fill the hole, the MOF finally obtained a "consumption"

or "value-added tax" in 1988. To make it more palatable, the rate was a low 3 percent, small businesses were exempt and companies could calculate their own taxes (and pocket some of the revenue while so doing). Yet, even that did not go down smoothly. In fact, there was a taxpayers revolt which brought down the government of Prime Minister Takeshita, who had billed the tax as the basis for creating an affluent and caring society. This left fiscal reform faint and farcical.

While the bureaucrats apparently preferred raising taxes, the businessmen pressed for an alternative approach, namely a reduction in expenditures. They feared that increased taxes would sap Japan's competitiveness. They were also annoyed that bureaucrats engaged in little belt-tightening in difficult times and showed marked inefficiency in many activities. At the behest of the Japan Federation of Economic Organizations (Keidanren), an administrative reform was introduced in 1982 and further intensified when Prime Minister Nakasone came to power. Keidanren's head, Toshiwo Doko, led the special committee which issued numerous recommendations to merge public bodies, reduce their budgets and decrease the number of personnel. Yet, after years of fitful efforts, little came of administrative reform either.[8]

So much for supremely competent financial, monetary and fiscal policy. The Japanese were only superior during easy periods. Whenever the crunch came, they were less impressive. And this is a cause for worry as the last and perhaps worst failure becomes visible. That is the amazing lack of preparation for the next century, when health and social security costs will balloon with a rapidly aging population, probable decrease in savings rates, and uncertain tax base.

Rearranging The Economy

Much of Japan's growth, as has already been explained, derived from export orientation as opposed to domestic demand.

This means that it sold more to foreigners than it bought from them and this differential increased the growth rate. That any such phenomenon existed was frequently denied by the Japanese government and foreign apologists, who pointed out that Japan exported less as a share of GDP than other nations or, in the inapt comparison of one observer, imported more than Great Britain (a country half its size).[9] But this did not change the embarrassing fact that over the years Japan's trade surplus continued rising, reaching a whopping $96 billion for 1987.

This left its trading partners with huge deficits. The biggest was incurred by the United States. It was naturally blamed on American inefficiency, shoddy goods, unwillingness to tackle the Japanese market, short-termism and whatever else occurred to its opponents. But it was not only the United States which could not penetrate the Japanese market. The Europeans did not do that much better and ran rather nasty deficits. So did the East Asian NICs whose imbalance with Japan was even larger proportionately. The only countries which could balance trade or show a surplus were oil producers.

Thus, there were evidently other reasons for this difficulty. Initially, they included relatively high tariffs and rather numerous quotas. Under foreign pressure, these were largely eliminated by the 1970s. Behind them, however, there were nontariff barriers which served much the same purpose. After denying they even existed, by the early 1980s, Japan conceded that they, too, should be scrapped. Yet, products still had trouble getting in. This drew attention to the distribution system, which was complex, and inter-company relations, which inhibited imports. In particular, the existence of groups or *keiretsu* encouraged Japanese companies to do business with one another rather than with foreigners, even if foreign products were as good and also cheaper.[10]

Naturally, while peeling away layer after layer of trade

Export-oriented? Who? Us?

Credit: Foreign Press Center/Kyodo

barriers, most countries could not afford to continue importing Japanese products which not only deterioriated their trade balance but disrupted crucial industries and resulted in closures and unemployment. By the 1960s, the United States, followed by Europe, and joined more recently by East Asian countries like Korea and Taiwan, threw up their own barriers against Japanese imports. This took various forms, from crude prohibitions and bans to flexible quotas. To help Japan save face, this might be disguised as export restraint instead. Still, one way or the other, it was obvious that Japan could only continue exporting more if it were willing to import more.

It took a terribly long time for the message to sink in, decades in fact. And it was never properly learned by MITI, which was widely known as the "Ministry-Of-One-Way-Trade." Prime Minister Nakasone, however, realized that Japan could never establish positive and cooperative relations in other sectors until trade relations were more harmonious. To this end, he asked an advisory group under Haruo Maekawa, former Governor of the Bank of Japan, to propose measures that would restructure the economy to make it more open and compatible. The Maekawa Reports, issued in 1986–87, were called dramatic by Japan's friends at home and abroad. On paper, certainly they were. They urged a radical restructuring of the economy from export-orientation to growth based on domestic demand, more open markets, a substantial increase in consumption and additional public works to improve the standard of living.

In practice, however, the plan did not appeal to many economic bureaucrats and businessmen were too competitive to care where they made money. Being more accustomed to exporting, though, they were not going to give that up just to please foreign dignitaries. Yet, during the late 1980s, something happened that was often purported to be an implementation of the Maekawa plan intentionally or unintentionally.

Intentionally, the Japanese government did lower the interest rate to stimulate demand. It also liberalized financial markets. And it even promoted imports, launching various "buy foreign" campaigns and pressuring companies to procure more goods abroad. But the biggest reason why imports increased was a result of the 1985 Plaza Accord, imposed on Japan by its trading partners, and the celebrated *endaka*. With this, dollar-denominated products were suddenly very cheap and naturally more could be bought . . . even with the remaining trade barriers.

Consequently, imports increased significantly, exports actually decreased somewhat, and Japan's trade surplus began shrinking. Success! cried the Japanese bureaucrats, intimating that they had accomplished something when the yen's revaluation they had long fought was the main cause. Success! cried the Japanapologists, including even supposedly sober publications like *The Economist*, which claimed that "the year 1988 has been one in which the doors to Japan's closed market have been prised apart."[11] Bill Emmott of *The Economist* went even further in his analysis. "This swing in trade flows is such that it suggests that Japan's current-account surplus could disappear within the next few years."[12]

They were all rather hasty. Japan's trade surplus did sink, but only to $64 billion in 1990, a pretty hefty sum. And the explanations for this decline were not as heartening as had been hoped. The biggest increase in imports was traced to oil, which the Japanese were now using with unaccustomed abandon. Manufactured imports also rose, but largely due to faster growth. When growth slowed down, imports of manufactured goods did as well. Worse, exports began mounting again as Japanese manufacturers rationalized to get by with a heavier yen. Thus, the trade surplus turned upward again after a rather short interlude.

Those who concluded that Japan had actually restructured its economy proved terribly wrong. Worse, those who insisted that Japan was at least *capable* of restructuring may have been almost as wrong. Future efforts may actually fare no better than this ill-fated attempt. For Japanese manufacturers seem able to export at virtually any exchange rate, although it takes time to revamp production. The idea that, once they were producing more locally they would export less, proved false as transplants in America and Europe imported huge amounts of parts and supplies. Then, when they became more self-sufficient, they would be sending profits back home.

Alas, (possible) improvements in the trade deficits would only be replaced by growing payments deficits in Japan's partners. And this not only could but would lead to new conflicts. That would further aggravate complaints about Japan's investment policy, namely that it was unfairly buying foreign companies and real estate. The United States, which again suffered the brunt of Japanese trade and investment, was already running a payments deficit and actually had the world's biggest debts. There was also emerging animosity about the supposed "buying of America."

Over a decade ago, I wrote about the "never-ending trade war."[13] That was admittedly a bit of an exaggeration. Never is a terribly long time. But it has already been going on for over forty years with no hope of a conclusion. And it could actually expand and intensify as payments and investment conflicts join the inevitable trade conflicts.

NOTES

1. Chalmers Johnson, *MITI And The Japanese Miracle*, p. 21.
2. *The Economist*, May 27, 1967.
3. Ibid.
4. For more on planning, see *Jon Woronoff, The Japan Syndrome*, pp. 120–5.
5. For more on targeting, see William R. Nester, *Japanese Industrial Targeting*, and Woronoff, *Japanese Targeting*.
6. *Daily Yomiuri*, April 30, 1986.
7. See Woronoff, *Politics, The Japanese Way*, pp. 240–7.
8. Ibid, pp. 295–304.
9. Bill Emmott, *The Sun Also Sets*, p. 67.
10. See Michael R. Czinkota and Woronoff, *Unlocking Japan's Market*, pp. 31–74.
11. *The Economist*, December 17, 1988, p. 69.
12. Emmott, op. cit., p. vii.
13. See Woronoff, *World Trade War*.

4
The Little Train That Couldn't

The Mighty Locomotive

The Japanese economy is a very dynamic one, racing ahead like the high-speed "bullet" train, passing every other train on the tracks and always getting there first. This, at least, is the appearance. And, over a decade ago, I purposely compared the economy to the *shinkansen*. But I warned readers not to look only at the sleek and shiny locomotive but the cumbersome passenger and freight cars it had to pull along. They might then find it distinctly less impressive. While this image caught on, to judge by the number of times it has been quoted since, I am not sure that enough observers are viewing the whole train even now.

Obviously, the powerful locomotive is the manufacturing sector . . . or part of it. For not even in manufacturing is there much evenness in what is still a rather lopsided economic structure. Only a limited circle of industries is worthy of admiration. They include mainly those which are export-oriented, for that is where Japan faces serious competition. They are usually sectors which can be highly automated, which is increasingly necessary as labor costs rise. And they deliver products that can be generated in large quantities.

Fortunately for Japan, the list of these products remains

fairly long. They include chemicals and fibers, a broad range of consumer electronics, motorcycles and automobiles, semiconductors and computers, machinery and telecommunications gear. Still emerging are pharmaceuticals and biotechnology, new materials, robots and communications satellites and rockets. Basic materials like steel and other metals, however, seem to have already peaked although they remain strong.

In each of these areas, Japan came from behind. It lagged during the war and had to catch up very quickly when peace returned. Companies had to be reorganized, workers trained and new technologies acquired. This was often done by the entrepreneurs themselves, as for consumer electronics, motorcycles and automobiles. But sometimes the task appeared so daunting that the government intervened to support and direct the private sector's effort. This took the form of industrial policy or targeting, whereby massive amounts of money were pumped into strategic sectors, the domestic market was temporarily closed until companies became competitive and then they were helped again with exports. Now the focus has shifted mainly to assistance with R&D.

But government intervention could only be a stopgap. Companies had to survive and grow on their own. This they achieved, among other things, by becoming some of the world's most proficient manufacturers. They built huge, modern factories applying the latest technologies. These facilities were as large as possible to capture economies of scale and bring down production costs per unit. In addition, the best machinery was installed and carefully organized to speed and smooth the flow of parts and material. Workers were painstakingly trained not only to master the techniques but contribute useful ideas about how the job could be done better.

The first phase was one of catch-up, where the Japanese admittedly copied from foreigners. Yet, even then, they were quite innovative and frequently managed to get more work out of the same machinery and manpower than their foreign rivals. They also showed a genius for design and strove to make products smaller, thinner, cheaper and more accessible to a broader public. By the 1980s, they had caught up in most sectors and had to become pathbreakers. While winning few Nobel Prizes, Japanese researchers did come up with useful improvements and popular products and, by the 1990s, Japan determined the state of the art in numerous sectors.

The key to this success was quality. Not only could the Japanese produce better and cheaper than most, whatever they delivered showed fewer defects. This was useful for ordinary consumer goods. For the latest articles, it was vital. Semiconductors, satellites, computers, sophisticated consumer items like VCRs and HDTV had to be nearly flawless. Reduction of defects and pursuit of the impossible goal of "zero defects" became a passion that few foreigners understood and none could replicate.

From these remarks, and my writing on the subject, it must be clear that while I criticize many aspects of the Japanese economy, I admire the ability to manufacture certain products better than anyone else. How could it be otherwise?

Still, we have to remember that these comments only apply to one dimension of the economy, manufacturing. And the whole manufacturing sector only accounts for 26 percent of gross domestic product at present. Moreover, along with the admirable portions of manufacturing, there are others that are less praiseworthy, almost half the total. This means that the locomotive pulling the Japanese economy is not all that big.

More worrisome is that the locomotive has to pull ever more clumsy and burdensome passenger and freight cars. While the locomotive has been getting smaller, the rest of the train has been getting larger proportionately. Once manufacturing was over a third of the economy, and most of it was trim and tough. By now the driving force has been re-

Gross Domestic Product By Industry (%)

	1976	1982	1988
Primary	5.2	3.2	2.3
Secondary	37.7	35.3	34.9
Manufacturing	28.0	26.0	25.9
Construction	9.2	8.9	8.6
Tertiary	57.1	61.5	62.8
Commerce	15.7	15.9	14.0

Japan's switch from manufacturing to services; doing less of what it does well and more of what it does poorly.

Source: Bank of Japan

duced to half what it was. And the still vital portion of manufacturing has to drag along inefficient manufacturers, sloppy contractors, superfluous retailers and supercilious service businesses. Their share has not ceased growing, as the table clearly shows, and already accounts for about three-quarters of the train. No wonder it is slowing down!

The Cumbersome Wagons

As mentioned, steel, electronics, automobiles and other products which are known and admired worldwide are not the only things Japan produces. There is much more. And most of it leaves a less agreeable impression.

Some of these products are fairly rudimentary, a carryover from earlier times. They include any number of artisanal items like pottery, lacquerware, *kimonos* or *tatami* mats. They are quaint and do not amount to much. But Japan is also very backward when it comes to cement production, although it is one of the world's largest and most voracious consumers. Nor have its manufacturers proven especially proficient for most of the things needed to furnish a home, from carpets to furniture, from curtains to beds. Some of the household appliances, those sold in Japan and not abroad, are amazingly archaic, such as cold-water washers that are hardly automatic.

Considerably more serious is that some of Japan's erstwhile winners have become losers. The first batch of industries to be promoted after the war included some that were labor-intensive and have ceased being viable. Textiles immediately come to mind. Even worse are ordinary garments and footwear. Shipbuilding, once the spearhead of economic growth, passed through hard times as orders decreased and ever more went to Korea and Taiwan. Petrochemicals and aluminum, which should probably never have been targeted to begin with, went into terminal decline after the oil crises. Even some electronics equipment is phasing out or moving to developing countries, simple televisions, radios, cassette recorders, even VCRs. VCRs also gave the death blow to the once lively movie camera industry.

Gradually, these sectors are proving a drag on the economy since, rather than letting them decline or disappear, in keeping with the concept of ''throw-away industries,'' the government has been trying desperately to preserve or revive them. MITI has come up with one scheme after another to help producers and workers, behaving almost as poorly as other advanced countries.[1] Yet, every yen it spends has to be taken from some other, more worthy purpose.

But the waste is still not as bad as encountered almost as a matter of course in other sectors which collectively account for the bulk of production. There is construction, with about 9 percent of GDP. Then tertiary activities, a massive 63 percent, of which commerce's 14 percent is most significant. Even if agriculture only amounts to just over 2 percent nowadays, it is an uncommonly unproductive 2 percent.

The construction sector is very inefficient, compared not only to sophisticated manufacturing but construction in most other places. That is partly due to lack of land and small family homes, which remain popular. But it can also be traced to inadequate standardization, limited use of prefabrication and the persistance of old-fashioned, labor-intensive techniques. In addition, many of the structures are rather flimsy and could hardly withstand a generation of normal use, let alone a typhoon or earthquake. Yet, residential and commercial properties are terribly expensive in Japan, due more to collusion among builders than the actual cost of inputs.

The Japanese have long conceded that they are rather inefficient for services and the government has urged improvement. But there is little to show for the efforts. There are more software houses, leasing and factoring have increased, and some financial products are excellent. But, even for business services, there remains much to be desired. When it comes to personal services, the situation is dismal, most notably so for eating and drinking establishments. Fast food joints have come; but dinky bars and restaurants still abound.

Occasionally, like manufacturing, services reveal a split personality. Banking and securities are dominated by a small number of dynamic entities and, when it comes to products with mass appeal, they prove ruthlessly efficient. Products of lesser interest, or with smaller margins, are backward. This includes such simple things as checking (which would bring in less money than bank transfers) or changing foreign currency (slow, painful, and expensive). Worse is that many individuals cannot even get loans from a bank and have to resort to cutthroat loan sharks (*sarakin*) who used to charge 110 percent annual interest and can still demand 55 percent today, rates that would be condemned as usury in any civilized nation.

Nothing is more distressing than the distribution system because it has repeatedly been singled out, both by the Japanese authorities and foreign critics, as an impediment to lower prices and improved living standards (plus imports). Yet, although various measures were taken and policies adopted, and the sector supposedly passed through a "dis-

The Distribution "Revolution"

Number (thousands)	1958	1968	1978	1988
Wholesale Establishments	193	240	369	436
Wholesale Employees	1,551	2,697	3,673	4,328
Retail Establishments	1,245	1,432	1,674	1,620
Retail Employees	3,273	4,646	5,960	6,851
Distribution Employees	4,824	7,343	9,633	11,179

That's funny, I thought the aim was to have less establishments and employees, not more.
Source: Management & Coordination Agency,
Japan Statistical Yearbook

tribution revolution," there has been little improvement. Indeed, the situation is actually worse than before. Over the past two decades, as the table clearly shows, the number of wholesalers, retailers and employees have increased rather than decreasing. There are more department stores, super-stores, speciality stores, convenience stores, even discount stores, but goods still pass through too many hands, each grabbing its margin, and end up costing too much.[2]

If construction, services and distribution are the passenger and freight cars, then agriculture must be the caboose. Of all the sectors, none is more wasteful and costly than it. Yet, rather than intentionally reducing or just leaving it to its own devices, the authorities have made one extravagant effort after the other to promote it. This consisted, more purposefully, of trying to introduce new crops and diversify farm earnings. That was tried with cattle, citrus fruits, vegetables and flow-ers. But the primary crop, rice, was not phased out. Instead, due to improved techniques and guaranteed prices, more rice was harvested than could be eaten. The subsidies for these assorted efforts were considerably higher in Japan than the most profligate Western country.

Meanwhile, the basic problem, small farms, was ignored.

This meant that farmers were inherently uncompetitive and increased use of machinery made limited sense. Thus, in addition to subsidies, it was necessary to protect agricultural produce by keeping out imports from the vast farms and ranges of Australia, Canada and the United States. This naturally bloated prices to the consumer. What with subsidies, the cost of modernizing the sector, and losses to the consumer, agriculture was a heavy burden on the economy. That it generated over 2 percent of GDP is meaningless when you consider that it cost more than 2 percent of GDP to keep the sector going. In fact, a meticulous study of Japanese agriculture concluded that its real net value added was negative.[3]

A Two-Track Economy

Many foreign observers also view Japan's corporate community, to vary the image somewhat, as a network consisting largely of bullet trains. These are big, powerful, prestigious companies whose names have become household words not only at home but abroad. They are the Toyotas and Nissans, the Hitachis and Toshibas, the Mitsubishis and Mitsuis which have effectively projected their influence and dominated their industries. Some are No. 1 and the rest are not far behind.

True, there are many excellent companies in Japan. They are well organized, well managed, well financed and able to produce fine products at reasonable prices. They know how to sell at home and export abroad. They are not quite as flawless as some would have us believe but, compared to American or European companies, they are pretty good. And, having visited their factories and spoken to their chief executives, I also came away impressed and have vaunted their qualities. How could I do otherwise?

But, and this is a big BUT, these are not the only companies in Japan. Traveling along the tracks, next to and usually behind the *shinkansen,* there are quantities of older, rickety and sometimes rundown trains. They rev up their engines and they try their best to speed down the tracks, but they never get very far, very fast. This would not be terribly significant except for the fact that the smaller, weaker companies are the vast majority. They account for over 99 percent of all businesses and employ 80 percent of the total labor force.

With small-and-medium enterprises (*chusho-kigyo*) being so numerous and so pervasive, they cannot simply be neglected as most often happens in books on the Japanese economy. For, while making a vital contribution to economic growth, they are somewhat of a drag. That can already be seen from the fact that they only account for 68 percent of gross domestic product while the large companies (*dai-kigyo*) generate 32 percent. They are even less represented when it comes to exports.[4]

One reason, of course, is that the smaller companies are less well endowed with efficient machinery and large-scale plants. With less capital, workers accomplish less and often the labor force is second-rate, at least by Japanese standards. Thus, the labor productivity per employee amounts to only about half that of larger companies. They are also short of advanced technologies, too poor to acquire them and too backward to accomplish much R&D on their own. What they often get is second hand equipment and second hand technologies from related firms.

Not surprisingly, smaller companies show lower profits and have an unenviable net worth or debt/equity ratio. In simple terms, they earn less and subsequently have to borrow more, borrowings they are often hard pressed to repay. No wonder they are the first to go under when the economy turns down and during recessions hundreds of thousands disappear. This precariousness of the companies inevitably leads to a precariousness of those who work for them, both management and labor.

If this were the fault of small businesses, then one might feel that any weakness or backwardness was justified. However, in Japan's two-tiered economic structure (*keizai no niju-kozo*), that is hardly the case. The vast majority of small companies are subcontractors of larger companies which, to be perfectly frank, exploit them. They may show some respect for long-standing relations and help their weaker partners when possible. But, by and large, they take advantage of the situation. This has been demonstrated by every serious study of the relationship, every comprehensive survey and every report of the Small and Medium Enterprise Agency.[5]

Basically, larger companies use subcontractors to carry out activities or produce parts or articles that no longer interest them. These are usually less profitable operations or products. They are also more labor-intensive and unpleasant. Thus, subcontractors produce older consumer electronics or fabricate smaller parts of ships. Sometimes they work in the parent company's own factory, sending their employees to do dirty and degrading tasks like painting, greasing, repairing minor defects or just cleaning up after hours.

Naturally, subcontractors also try to get ahead by introducing improved techniques, adopting new technologies or acquiring better equipment. But this does little for their bottom line because the parent company, once it realizes they can produce more cheaply, demands that prices be cut. It exerts similar pressure whenever price competition occurs or it wishes to export more. In fact, the pressure for lower prices is unending. Worse, in most cases, subcontractors do not even get a fixed price for their output; it is always negotiable. Nor do they receive a written contract in most instances; they have to accept verbal commitments.

There is little that subcontractors can do to resist this

because, unlike the situation elsewhere, most of them only have one parent company or very few customers. They are too dependent on the buyer's good will to complain, let alone demand more. In addition, often enough, the parent company owns stock, places its men on the board, imposes former employees on the staff and, in general, keeps close watch and tight control. What would happen if the subcontractor does not meet expectations? It would be cast off and replaced by another, regretfully perhaps, but no less certainly.

This unequal arrangement is already an old one. Contemporary observers wrote of a dual economic structure a hundred years ago when Japan was first developing. The duality then appeared rooted in the difficult transition from a traditional to a modern economy. It should, in the view of many, gradually disappear. But it did not. Indeed, it has remained an indelible feature of the postwar period and has in some ways only gotten worse. It is therefore impossible to overlook it in considering Japan, no matter how hard the apologists try.

To improve the situation, it will take more than just increased investment or strenuous efforts because, as long as big companies dominate small ones, the latter gain relatively little. Yet, the government has done almost nothing to break the dependence. It has admittedly made token gestures. They consisted of financial aid, some protection, help with R&D and the like. A Small and Medium Enterprise Agency was created. But this was petty compared to what has been done for larger companies, often under targeting exercises, by the vastly more powerful Ministry of International Trade and Industry.

That is why one must be wary of the hackneyed and misleading story of government, whether through the Liberal Democratic Party or well-meaning bureaucrats, trying to correct the imbalance. It is hard to agree with Kent Calder, one of the rising apologists, in making claims like the following.

"One of the most striking features of recent Japanese public policy, viewed both in comparative context and against the backdrop of Japanese history, has been the fluctuating but generally pronounced bias shown toward the small, across a range of industrial, trade, and credit-policy sectors, often at the expense of the large."[6]

In short, the lot of the small company, and especially the small subcontractor, is not a happy one. That has been shown in great detail by the few books by foreigners that even bother describing the situation, one of the most interesting being Norma J. Chalmers' *Industrial Relations in Japan, The Peripheral Sector*. And it was confirmed by one of Japan's foremost experts on productivity, Joji Arai of the International Productivity Service.

"A lack of qualified employees, know-how, funds, sophisticated equipment and machinery, product knowledge, and market information will subjugate Japanese small companies to large businesses, inasmuch as they hope to attain independence. Small firms feel the strongest competitive pressure from emerging new industries of newly industrialized countries. They are also vulnerable to price fluctuations of raw materials and energy, as well as changes in marketplaces."[7]

Thus, anyone evaluating Japan's economy must not only consider both advanced and backward sectors but also advanced and backward companies. For the latter, the situation is even more skewed since these weaker firms vastly outnumber more sophisticated companies. And their fate seems to be getting worse rather than better. That goes a long way toward explaining not only why Japan's economy is no longer as strong as before but why it is still slowing down.

NOTES

1. See Woronoff, *Targeting*, pp. 192–210.
2. See Czinkota and Woronoff, *Unlocking Japan's Market*, pp. 111–40.
3. Cornelius L.J. Van Der Meer and Saburo Yamada, *Japanese Agriculture: A Comparative Economic Analysis*.
4. See annual *White Papers* of Small and Medium Enterprise Agency.
5. See Norma J. Chalmers, *Industrial Relations in Japan, The Peripheral Workforce*, and Michael J. Smitka, *Competitive Ties, Subcontracting in the Japanese Automotive Industry*.
6. Kent Calder, *Crisis and Compensation*, p. 312.
7. Joji Arai, "Technology's Impact on Small Businesses in Japan," *International Productivity Journal*, Winter 1991.

5
Japan's Wasted Workers

Productivity Peters Out

Many fawning observers attribute Japan's success to that good old-fashioned virtue hard work. "It is not surprising," they say, "that Japan has done so well when its labor force works so hard."

By now it should be generally known that it is not "hard work" as such that brings about economic development. No matter how hard you work, if you only accomplish as much today as yesterday your economy will not grow. In fact, it is more likely to blossom once you stop working hard and start working smart. That is, when brute human labor is replaced by something else. The "something else" can be more and better machinery and equipment. It can involve a more intelligent use of whatever machine and manpower is applied. It can occur when the same inputs are used to create other, more attractive products.

Thus, "hard work" has never been an explanation of Japan's economic advance or anybody else's. This must be hard work suitably applied. To be fair, the Japanese have done an excellent job of getting more out of each man hour of labor than most. Indeed, during the 1950s and 1960s they managed to boost productivity at rates that appeared quite miraculous, often soaring above 10 percent a year. This put them well ahead of less imaginative Europeans and apparently lazier Americans. But this edge has been decreasing over time. By the 1970s, Japan's productivity was only rising somewhat faster than that of other OECD members and, by the 1980s, it was only marginally higher. Meanwhile, it was markedly outpaced by the newly industrialized countries.

There are various reasons for this. One is that it was becoming increasingly difficult to find superior machinery or sophisticated technology that could boost output by substantial increments. It was also harder to improve the design of factories that were already state-of-the-art or fine tune work practices that had repeatedly been refined over the years. This was already serious. What made it even more worrisome was that, just when productivity growth was slowing down, wages were climbing to American and European levels and appreciably higher than in other East Asian countries.

This meant that even "hard work" would not be enough for Japan to maintain an edge in all manufacturing sectors. There were still some where the Americans or Europeans, using more capital or better techniques, were ahead. There were others where East Asians, combining cheaper (and sometimes yet harder-working) labor and ever more capital had caught up. Comparative studies showed that, while outperforming for steel, electronics and automobiles, there were other areas where Japan was only just as good or less productive. Even for overall manufacturing productivity, according to the Japan Productivity Council, Japan still lagged behind some European countries and the United States which had a level of 112 compared to Japan's 100 in 1987.[1]

That was in manufacturing, the sector Japan concentrated on almost to the exclusion of others. When you consider the economy as a whole, Japan's productivity compared even less favorably. Rather than a leader, it was a laggard in most places. In agriculture, its performance was horrible.

But it was hardly brilliant in distribution, transportation or construction and even finance left much to be desired. Taking one thing with another, Japan was no productivity hero. Its overall rating in 1987 was only 100 compared to 134 in the United States and lesser margins elsewhere. In fact, according to the JPC, it was next-to-last among eleven members of the Organization for Economic Cooperation and Development.

So much for the idea that the Japanese work "hard," let alone harder than everyone else. Or the idea that they work smarter, use better equipment and techniques or come up with superior products . . . across the board. The same dichotomy we have seen between the economic performance of various sectors applies to productivity and the use of labor. In manufacturing, this is (usually) excellent. Elsewhere, it is (frequently) mediocre.

There is a second dichotomy, this one related to the dual structure. In all sectors, larger companies tend to be considerably more productive than smaller. This is most visible in manufacturing where smaller firms use less machinery, older machinery, poorer techniques, and so on. Productivity is about twice as high in larger companies, on the whole, than smaller companies. Productivity is also much higher for those products which can be manufactured in great quantities using the latest techniques. Those produced in smaller quantities do not benefit nor do certain processes which are harder to automate. These, by the way, are usually relegated to smaller suppliers or subcontractors, which helps explain their low levels of productivity.

More surprising is that, even in the very same companies that boast extraordinary levels of productivity on the shop floor, productivity in the office is comparatively poor. This is one of my supposedly unfriendly messages that has gotten through and was more broadly explained in *Japan's Wasted Workers* and more recently *The Japanese Management Mys-*

Comparative Productivity 1987

	Japan	United States	Germany	France
Manufacturing	100	112	84	87
Agriculture, forestry and fishery	100	337	135	226
Construction	100	118	135	142
Wholesale and retail	100	167	137	171
Transportation and communication	100	155	128	131
Finance, insurance and real estate	100	119	98	127
Overall	100	134	124	131

How can you manufacture so well and do everything else so poorly?

Source: Japan Productivity Center, *International Comparison of Productivity Level and Trends of 11 OECD Countries*, 1989.

tique.[2] Now it is almost common knowledge that blue-collar workers and white-collar employees behave quite differently within the Japanese system. Just how differently will be explored in the next section. How workers in agriculture, distribution and services, to say nothing of government bureaucrats, can be wasted even more lamentably is shown in two other sections.

This should clarify why Japan's productivity growth, and consequently economic growth, have been less vigorous in recent years. It should also intimate why the future prospects are not that bright. For the high productivity sector, manufacturing, is a dwindling share of the whole. Other sectors account not only for considerably more output but also more labor, and they are growing. This means there will be more and more inefficient workers and less and less efficient ones, unless something drastic—and rather unexpected—occurs.

Contrast In Blue And White

The positive image of Japan's workers can probably be traced to what is known of the factory workers, especially those in larger companies. There is no question but that they work hard. Too hard, sometimes, to judge by the number of ailments that afflict them and the limited free time they enjoy.

For one, productivity gains have been wrung out of them by making them do ever more during the same time. Workers are expected to carry out more specific tasks, in less time, than elsewhere. When they reach that goal, they are asked to do more. Five workers are pushed to accomplish what was previously done by six and, when that is achieved, four workers have to do it. Meanwhile, tasks that could be finished in 30 seconds next have to be done in 25, and doubtlessly later in 20. The pace of the assembly line is steadily accelerated and if it goes too fast, and a worker makes a mistake, he has to pull an alarm so the rest of the staff knows.

As if that were not enough, workers are supposed to show devotion to the company. That means, among other things, that they arrive early to set out their equipment and get in position. They cut their coffee and lunch breaks short to do a bit more work. And they have to leave late, after having neatly put their tools in place and prepared work for the next day. This may seem fair. It is probably less so that workers do not always work by the clock but the job. They pledge to produce so many units a day and, if that quota is not met, they have to put in "voluntary" overtime to get the job done. Meanwhile, during the day, there is not a moment's relaxation because, as noted, every second is accounted for.

Workers also work smarter, whether they want to or not. Industrial engineers and supervisors see to that. Personnel is positioned so that more can be accomplished in less time and the time-and-motion boys are there to check. Equipment is adapted to the needs, making work easier but also more ef-

Foreigners gawking at super-efficient factories.

Credit: JNTO

ficient. When a worker is not fast or accurate enough, he is simply replaced by a machine or robot. For all the lip service paid to workers, there is no compunction about dropping them if they cannot keep up.

In addition, factory workers are expected to contribute to productivity by coming up with their own ideas. This is done partly through the quality control movement and similar exercises, some with exaggerated goals like zero defects. After hours, workers get together and discuss their tasks, to see exactly what they are doing and why, and then devise ways of improving. This is not voluntary by any means. All the workers are not only supposed to show up but participate actively. They also have to make suggestions, not when they feel so moved, but so many a month or year. Less than total commitment would be held against them.

Quality control, productivity campaigns, suggestion boxes and the like are often regarded as the explanation of Japan's high productivity. That is not true. Just like every other economy, the biggest gains have come from using more and better machinery. According to an acknowledged authority, Hajime Ohta, "the large increase in labor productivity improvement in the 1960s and the early 1970s is largely attributable to the increase in capital investment that resulted in more equipment per worker."[3] If the Japanese were still using the old machinery, no matter how hard or smart they worked, they would not be very productive.

That is what happens in the factory. The situation is mind-boggingly different in the office, the habitat of the salaried employee or "salaryman" (*sarari-man*). There, things are not organized strictly and efficiently, employees are not straining to get their work done on time, nor are they busily figuring out how to improve from day to day and year to year. That much is visible to the naked eye.

Let's start with the idea of each worker in his place doing his job as best he can. As the next section will show in greater detail, most white-collar employees do not have specific jobs. Nor do they have specific posts. Rather, they tend to work on tasks collectively and allocate tasks as they go along, rather than follow clearly defined procedures. While they do have desks, these are all placed in a large room with little privacy and little peace and quiet, so they remain exposed to all that is going on around them. A person's location, moreover, is not a function of what he does but where he ranks in the pecking order, with senior employees located closer to the boss and junior ones further out, while many of the women are somewhere in limbo.

Amazingly enough, relatively little is done in the way of enhancing productivity through capital investment. Floor workers have ever more efficient machines and designers use computer-aided techniques. Yet white-collar employees have little familiarity with or respect for computers. Unlike many Western companies, where each person has a computer on the desk, and uses it regularly, Japanese offices often place all the computers off in a corner where they are serviced by female subordinates.

This new-fangled gadgetry is not for the men. Indeed, as I pointed out, many operate as if the telephone had not yet been invented. Rather than discuss problems over the phone and only meet personally for important matters or to finalize decisions, the salarymen constantly engage in meetings. There are meetings with counterparts in the same section, between different sections, with clients, with suppliers, with government officials, and so on. Given the painstaking decision-making process, this can occur repeatedly and last indefinitely. This low level of efficiency is further depressed by lengthy travel times.

Obviously, none of this contributes to working smarter. But office workers do not even make the effort of their colleagues in the factory. There are no productivity drives or QC circles for the salarymen. They are not expected to submit suggestions regularly. That would be beneath them. Attempts by audacious companies to change this have had only limited results and most of the QC is done by lower-level or female personnel, especially those with simple, routine tasks.

While this can be comprehended, if not necessarily condoned, it is hard to find anything nice to say about one last aspect of productivity, namely intensity of work. There is no question that Japanese office employees put in long hours, arriving early, sometimes staying in for lunch, and then leaving late. This has earned them a reputation as "workaholics." But not much of that time is actually work. It may just be a semblance of work or, more often than suspected, plain goofing off.

Indeed, should anyone appear unexpectedly in a Japanese office, as I have frequently done, he would find many salarymen doing nothing that even remotely resembles work. He would see employees sitting around reading newspapers, watching television, leafing through comics or travel brochures, playing cards, sipping tea or whatever. They usually do this in the presence of their superior, who is at least making an effort to look busy, his desk piled high with papers, but may just be killing time by consulting earnestly with one subordinate or another.

If the men are goofing off, it is hard to define exactly what the women are doing. For many of them have supposed "jobs" which are not even intended to be purposeful or productive. Often the "office ladies" or OLs just copy papers, type form letters, deliver messages, tidy up desks, or serve tea. The more glorified ones now act as assistants of a sort, answering the phone for superiors but not making decisions. And some have graduated from the typing pool to the computer pool. Yet, on the whole, they are just there to brighten up the office, which is why they are still described as the "flower of the office" (*shokuba no hana*).

On the face of it, it is hard to see how office workers can get away with this while factory workers keep their nose to the proverbial grindstone. The reason probably has to do with hierarchy or even caste. Factory workers are by and large just high school graduates, less educated individuals in a society whose pecking order is based on education. They can be given orders, moved around at will and expected to engage in relatively monotonous or unpleasant tasks. Moreover, in the factory it is much easier to supervise them closely and measure accurately what each one is doing.

In the office, especially with the lack of specific jobs and periodic rotations, it is hard to even tell who is working efficiently and who is not. Thus, evaluation is partly based on an appearance of activity and devotion, one which is easy enough to simulate. The key, however, is that office workers (including most OLs) are college graduates. They are part of

What would foreigners think of the office?

Credit: Mitsubishi Corp.

the higher caste and some of them will rise to the top of the organization. It would be unseemly to impose a similar discipline on them. And most such attempts have been rejected. Nor can the more educated employees be readily conned into working harder or smarter by management.

Japan's Renowned (Mis)management System

These are relatively surface, but no less significant, phenomena and help explain why Japan's success is due more to what is happening in the factories than what is going on in the offices. But they are grafted on a management system that has been widely acclaimed in the West, largely by gurus who admire but scarcely understand it. There is no question that many of the features are helpful and constructive, but not all, and even the better aspects leave much to be desired. This has been realized by Japanese managers, workers and management experts.[4]

The basis of much of what happens is the so-called "career escalator," which is a crucial element of the reputed "lifetime employment" system. New recruits get on at the bottom and are gradually carried upward, from year to year, gaining promotions and higher wages along the way. This instills greater loyalty in them, since they are part of the company and know that they should be able to ride the escalator to the top. Since they are all on the same escalator, a variation on the theme of "all in the same boat," they will pull together for the company's success. They will also get to know the company extremely well, much better than employees of Western companies where people come and go.

But there are also disadvantages. Some affect the individual worker, who may not be challenged as much or may find he is not rewarded for special efforts. Others affect the company's performance. Both sides are summed up very nicely by Kunio Odaka, one of Japan's leading industrial sociologists.

"Under the escalator system, even if an ambitious person applies his special talents to achieve major accomplishments, the corporation takes almost no direct notice of his feats. . . . To the outstanding employee who knows that he has special talents and has achieved special results, the exaggerated impartiality of the company can only be a source of dissatisfaction. As time passes and this dissatisfaction festers, the employee loses the desire to do outstanding work or to contribute any more of himself to the company than he has to. The result is that the system creates a large number of outwardly efficient but inwardly mediocre and lazy company men who are 'never idle, never late, but never actually working.' This is detrimental not only to the employee with outstanding abilities but also the company as a whole."[5]

Other problems arise from the fact that, for the most part, salaried employees are hired as generalists. They have not developed any specialties while in college or, even if they did, that is not regarded as particularly important. They are hired more for their personality and ability to adapt than their knowledge, if any. They are then allocated to the various sections and divisions where they are given assignments advertising, personnel, production and so on that would normally be done by specialists in the West. There are some specialists in Japan, but much fewer, and they are stuck in relatively narrow slots while the generalists are the fast-track employees who will make it to the top.

This would not be so bad if not for the fact that, to round out the generalists' experience, they are rotated from job to job every two or three years. And the new job may not be even vaguely related to the old. Thus, during an initial period they must learn the tasks, for which they may have little aptitude or ability. And, anyway, two or three years is not much time to acquire expertise. Then, as rotation time approaches, they lose interest since they will soon be working at completely different tasks with different people.

Again, this would not be so bad if not for the fact that what they are supposed to do in each position is very poorly defined. In many cases, there is no job description and the new man is simply expected to take over whatever was being done by his predecessor. Frequently, rather than work at a specific task on his own he becomes part of a team which as a whole accomplishes many assorted tasks. Just what is expected of each team member is quite obscure aside from the need to pitch in with vigor. Thus, there is much duplication and overlap plus occasional gaps.

To sort things out, salarymen resort to time-honored practices which are not in themselves very efficient. Best known, because most popularized by foreign management gurus, are assorted meetings and *ringi-seido*. Meetings are called interminably, at all levels, and involving anyone even remotely concerned. They are usually quite lengthy and more often than not inconclusive. Actually reaching a decision is hampered by the need to obtain not a majority view, let alone action imposed by a strong leader, but a broad consensus. To bring everyone in, sponsors may engage in an endless round of one-on-one consultations quaintly described as "root binding" or *nemawashi*.

Much is made of bottom-up decision-making (as opposed to top-down giving of instructions in the West). This is accomplished by having junior staff draw up *ringisho* or proposals which are then gradually channeled upwards. Each superior either puts his stamp on it as approved or fails to do so, hinting that he does not agree. When it finally reaches the top, and is accepted, the underlings can do what they want . . . if they remember what it was. For the process can take not weeks or months but years and is hardly adapted to quick action.

These practices can easily degenerate, with one meeting calling forth another, and one proposal eliciting a counterproposal and all this "action" actually being inaction. The outcome may be not decision but indecision. Or, perhaps even worse, decisions that nobody is responsible for because everybody was responsible. They can also become a mere ritual, as even a supporter of the system conceded. "Anybody with an idea puts it in a *ringisho*. Anybody with pride wants to be on its circulation list. The result is a ritual dance of circulating and approving that has nothing whatsoever to do with meaningful work."[6]

This ritual can be particularly futile when you consider that often the consensus is not spontaneous but contrived. First off, junior employees would not make proposals they expected their superiors to reject. Rather, they would first feel them out and suggest something generally acceptable. If there were resistance, the proposal would be withdrawn or just die. More insidious, often senior staff feed ideas to their juniors so that it would appear that these ideas arise further down. Anyway, and this will make Western gurus gasp, according to a recent survey of company presidents by *Toyo Keizai*, there is actually more top-down than bottom-up management in Japan.[7]

Subsidies and Services

It is no longer necessary to argue that Japan's agricultural sector is hopelessly inefficient. That is already conceded by everybody, including the Ministry of Agriculture. Its 1990 White Paper indicated that productivity was only one fourth as high as in manufacturing. And that was overly generous. If you consider that Japan's producer prices are four times higher than import prices, according to agricultural researcher Kunitaro Takeda, agricultural productivity is really only one-sixteenth as high.[8]

This abysmally low productivity can be attributed to numerous factors, too many to mention all of them here. Just the major ones follow.

First of all, plots of land are too small to be farmed efficiently. The average size plot is merely about one hectare, which is not just infinitely smaller than American or Australian farms but even small compared to those in Europe. Many of them are also on marginal land of dubious fertility and unfavorable climate. Yet, the Japanese continue farming them as long as they can get four and more times the world price for most crops. If faced by genuine competition, like manufacturers, most farmers would go out of business or have to rationalize . . . which would not be a bad thing. After all, if land were consolidated into larger plots, farms could be run more productively.

That is not only because larger spaces would increase the land tended by each farmer. For once, he would be getting proper value out of his machinery. Low productivity is not due to lack of machinery since the Japanese, thanks to pushy equipment makers, overeager cooperatives and government subsidies, manage to acquire one of each. They also use more fertilizers and chemicals than other farmers. If anything, they use too much capital for the size of their farms. With larger farms, and proportionately less machinery and inputs than today, they could produce more for less.

Finally, there are simply too many "fake" farmers. Of the three million supposed farmers, only half-a-million live solely from the land. The rest have jobs in manufacturing or services and only look after their miniature plots on weekends. In addition, the real farmers are growing old. Many are already old enough to retire, except that nobody in the family is willing to take over the job. This means that, even if they had larger farms, they would not be interested in farming them efficiently. They are too set in their ways or too tired to try something new and which will not pay off for years.

Distribution, as was already noted, is quite inefficient as well. That is for some of the same reasons. Just as there are too many farms, there are also too many shops, many of them far smaller than outlets in other countries. Not surprisingly, the smaller retailers are inefficient. But wholesalers, which could boost efficiency more readily, continue supplying them at great cost and inconvenience. They must deliver tiny lots, at frequent intervals, to keep the shelves full. Only as larger stores replace smaller ones can productivity be enhanced. Yet, despite a much touted distribution "revolution," there has not been a decrease in the number of outlets since new ones added to, rather than replacing, old ones.

Still, it would be assumed that with modern merchandising techniques, the outlets could at least operate more efficiently and absorb less personnel. As the statistics show, that was also not the case. There are more people employed in distribution than ever. That is because efficiency regularly takes second place to "service." This attention to service has traditional roots but remains strong, as expressed in the saying that the "customer is God" (*okyakusama wa kamisama desu*).

Thus, retailers make lavish use of personnel as salesgirls, shop assistants, floor managers and the like. In more plush establishments, it is not just a question of meeting the customers' need so much as making them feel good. There are uniformed girls to operate the elevators, others to usher shoppers onto the escalators, and enough staff at each counter that one never has to wait. Even modest purchases are neatly wrapped and special ones consume prodigious amounts of paper and ribbons. Many department stores still deliver ordinary gifts while high class shops now have "tuxedo boys" to bring gifts to the recipient's home.

But it is not only stores that use personnel wastefully, automakers do the same. Most of the business does not come from potential purchasers visiting the showroom, as in the West. Rather, salesmen (*serusuman*) are sent out to visit former or prospective clients. They will go to their home once, twice, three times and more to make a sale. After the sale, even if there is nothing wrong with the car, they will phone in, send cards or make personal visits. For the customers' birthday, fruit and cakes are delivered. This adds immensely to the cost of doing business, and cuts into the automakers' profits, but they do not seem able to throw the habit.

The service industry is not that very different. There are far too many small establishments, each with its own premises and personnel, and many unable to boost productivity in any sensible manner. They all use too much personnel. That much is obvious for those that emphasize "service," like restaurants, bars or night clubs. But even banks have bevies of girls, each in a cute uniform, to bow and smile to the customer (while some man in the back does the actual work). Meanwhile, securities and insurance companies send out veritable armies of sales personnel to prospect for business from door to door.

In many instances, the main cause of inefficiency is "service," which implies an excessive use of personnel. In this way, Japan differs from many other countries, not only Western but also Asian, where price is equally or more important. Moreover, service usually involves doing all sorts of unnecessary things for the customer (like bowing over the escalator), things they could do themselves (like visit a showroom) or don't really need (like the little gifts distributed by banks). Until price does rank more highly, there is little hope that productivity will rise. And, since service has implied wasteful use of personnel for centuries already, change will take time.

In a more impersonal sector like construction, where service does not play as big a role, you would expect Japan to be more efficient. After all, its contractors are renowned worldwide for putting up huge projects, involving thousands of units, at the lowest possible cost through use of highly advanced technologies. Not in Japan. There, they prefer handling small projects or building houses one at a time, each one differently. Part of the problem is the lack of land, which makes it hard to find big enough plots for major projects. Another is that the plots are often oddly shaped so the building has to be tailored to the space. Then, of course, it is not hard to convince buyers that they are special and should have a special home.

That is only the start. Contractors often use rather old-fashioned, time-consuming techniques such as putting up small homes with costly "post-and-beam" methods rather than prefabricating more. And the work is not done by organized construction teams but through subcontracting. Those who get the job simply hire smaller firms to handle the work, which in turn recruit yet smaller firms, which depend on tiny firms with only a few workers for certain chores. The use of manpower is extravagant in a country where manpower is in

Structure of Employment

Year	Composition (%)		
	Primary	Secondary	Tertiary
1950	48	22	30
1960	30	28	42
1970	17	35	48
1980	10	35	55
1990	7	34	59

More and more to "service" what less and less produce.

Source: Bank of Japan

short supply and thus expensive. But, since they get a cut on each layer, the system meets the needs of the builders if not those of the buyers.

Once again, it must be stressed that it is not merely a question of inefficiency and wasting workers in some few small sectors. To the contrary, the bulk of the labor force is engaged in the areas just described. Agriculture, while producing little GDP, still employs 7 percent. Construction, which is included under secondary sectors, has some 9 percent. And the tertiary sector, the largest and still growing, consists of distribution and services, the bulk of its nearly 60 percent of the labor force.

Ballot Boxes And Red Tape

There is one other category of workers who are frequently wasteful and occasionally wasted, namely the political leadership. In Japan, due to a strange symbiosis, this implies both the politicians and the bureaucrats. Both clans are unusually numerous, costly and of uncertain value.

Japan is a small, tight and pretty homogeneous country. Its people are relatively docile and obedient. One would think that it would be fairly easy to govern such a country and that this could be done with rather few politicians. Instead, as it turns out, Japan has proportionately more politicians than most other countries, including the United States with its vast spaces, regional differences, mixed ethnic composition and individualistic characters. In fact, the lower house of the Japanese Diet has 512 members as opposed to 435 in the American House of Representatives.

This bloated personnel structure exists at lower levels as well. Despite its modest size, Japan is divided into 47 prefectures, almost as many as American states. Each one has its own government and so do all the smaller localities, including cities, towns, villages and hamlets. In addition, at each level, there is a tendency to have more elected officials on prefectural assemblies or town councils than similar bodies in other countries. Very roughly, there are about twice as many politicians in Japan as the United States, with twice the population, which works out to four times as many politicians per person.

Not only are there more of them, they are paid higher wages and receive more generous perks than most of their counterparts abroad.[9] In fact, salaries are quite decent even compared to Japanese bureaucrats and businessmen. As for the perks, they are sometimes outrageous to judge by the number of politicians eating in exclusive restaurants, riding about in chauffeur-driven limousines and making expensive junkets abroad. To top it all off, they spend considerable state monies on handsome, sometimes even resplendent, public buildings, such as the Tokyo Metropolitan Government offices in Shinjuku.

These are only the visible costs. Invisible ones exist as well. Most prominent are the expenses of holding electoral campaigns which, for the Diet at least, are very frequent due to periodic, unnecessary cabinet reshuffles. National elections occur about every two years although there is no need to hold them more than once in four years. Costs are exorbitant, especially for candidates in the ruling party, and now run about ¥1 billion a seat.[10] The total amount spent on these exercises is hard to estimate but clearly runs into the trillions.

In order to cover this, and other current expenditures, the political parties are forever raising funds, and actually increasing the kitty over the years. The total collected in 1990 was ¥337 billion, another record high. But that only included the sums that were duly reported. Substantial amounts, certainly enough to double that figure, pass surreptitiously between politicians and their backers in business or pressure groups. Some politicians also round out their take with illicit gifts and kickbacks.

What do the politicians do to merit this largesse? That is rather hard to say. Normally, politicians prepare legislation, debate and adopt or reject it, and supervise the execution of laws. That is not the case in Japan.[11] There, the bureaucrats draw up the bills, coach ministers on how to present and defend them, and then implement laws which they tend to adapt and modify as they see fit. Senior politicians in the ruling Liberal Democratic Party have some input in the process, but not terribly much. As for the opposition members, they frequently object verbally but rarely block legislation.

Nonetheless, politicians are extremely busy. Some of this activity is devoted to governing, but not much. More consists of keeping the folks in the constituency happy, not so much by shaping legislation but attending to petty needs like gifts for weddings, gifts for funerals, gifts for assorted gift-giving festivities. This is needed to obtain support for the most important task of all, running for frequent elections and getting elected often enough to hold on to the job and rise in the pecking order.

The real work of governing, as noted, has been largely assumed by the bureaucracy. They are, of course, not entitled to do so by the Constitution. But the politicians are so busy that somebody has to do the job and they feel that as an educational and traditional elite, that is their responsibility. They also benefit palpably from this. Not so much with regard to pay, since bureaucratic wages are relatively modest, as an ironclad "lifetime" job. Moreover, as the true power brokers, shaping legislation and allocation of state monies, they can make influential friends in business or public corporations who will offer them cushy *amakudari* posts when they retire. Since they retire young, about fifty, they have plenty of time to reap the harvest.

While the bureaucrats are essential in governing Japan, and administration would come to a halt without them, there is reason to question just how much they are worth.

First of all, there is a very large number of bureaucrats, not only at the national but also the various local levels. In this case, the total payroll is somewhat less than in other advanced countries. On the other hand, they have less to do since the schools are undermanned, law and order is less troubled, and especially the welfare facilities are modest in the extreme. For that, it is hard to see why Japan needs 4.5 million national and local employees or some 7 percent of the total workforce.

What is actually of greater concern is not how many bureaucrats there are but how they are distributed. In Japan, the pecking order changes very slowly if at all. The older, more prestigious ministries remain the largest whether or not that is justified by their responsibilities. Thus, although MITI no longer has to promote new sectors, protect domestic industry or regulate many areas, its staff has hardly decreased. The same applies to MOF. Even more inflated is the Ministry of Agriculture, which still has one of the biggest staffs and is looking after a sector that has not ceased shrinking. On the other hand, there is a dire need of more educational and welfare facilities, but a shortage of personnel in both fields.

Naturally, where there is excess, even plethoric personnel, bureaucrats will look for things to do. Some of these things may be helpful, others are superfluous, and quite a few just get in the way. Thus, although industry can develop on its own, MITI still comes up with research projects or helps out those sectors which are in trouble, a costly and usually wasteful task. MOF, having deregulated financial services, tries to control them through other forms of administrative guidance. The Ministry of Agriculture keeps on introducing new crops, none of which fare very well.

In general, all of the bureaucrats have a penchant for red tape. This goes far back and, since ordinary citizens have limited clout, rules and regulations proliferate. Most of them just make it harder and costlier to do things that are, in principle at least, permitted. For example, opening a new store required 73 applications, for 28 separate approvals, under 12 different laws.[12] But the bureaucrats need this to justify their existence, retain control over the citizenry and earn points with potential future employers when they smooth the way through this thicket of regulations.

Equally unpleasant, although they work shorter hours and have more weekends off, many bureaucrats tend to come late and leave early, expand their lunch break and, in general, laze around rather than concentrate on work . . . to judge by irate letters to the editor. They are anything but efficient in processing requests and apparently enjoy making commoners wait. Internally, enormous time is wasted in meetings to agree on action. Much of this is devoted to harmonizing relations not only between ministries or departments but within them as opposed to accommodating politicians or the broader public. Aside from that, according to the man and woman in the street, they remain inordinately arrogant.

This sort of featherbedding and make-work is extremely wasteful if hard to measure in monetary terms. Still, it is obvious that government ministries and agencies were spending more than they should for what they got, none being more profligate than the Defense Agency. It regularly had military equipment, even planes and tanks produced locally at two, three and four times the cost of buying foreign material. Meanwhile, year after year, the Board of Audit revealed billions of taxpayers' yen wasted or misused in all parts of the administration. Even on the local level, the authorities were spending more for garbage disposal, school lunches or ordinary personnel than the private sector.

It might be hoped that public corporations, run along more businesslike lines, would be more efficient. Usually, they were not. This was partly because they were subject to political imperatives, partly because they did not have to make profits. The worst example was the national railway system, which built one *shinkansen* line after the other. True, the bullet trains were faster, but the cost of building them was huge and the new lines made older ones obsolete. The result was a ¥26 trillion debt. The telephone and telegraph monopolies were not quite as profligate, but hardly profitable. Meanwhile, the many entities created to build public works barely knew the meaning of cost efficiency.

Why has the bureaucracy been so inefficient? Aside from the weaknesses to which all bureaucracies are subject, Japan's problem stems from the fact that the bureaucrats have too much control over the politicians, and the public has too little control over the politicians and bureaucrats, to keep them in line. Only the business community could conceivably do something. It also had a reason to intervene, namely the steadily mounting cost of government which demanded ever more taxes. During the 1980s, business leaders actively sought administrative reform. But, as noted, there was not much to show for those efforts.

NOTES

1. Japan Productivity Center, *International Comparison of Productivity Levels and Trends in 11 OECD Countries*, 1989.

98

2. On these subjects, see Jon Woronoff, *Japan's Wasted Workers* and *The Japanese Management Mystique.*
3. Hajime Ohta, "Productivity Growth in Japan—The Last Twenty Years," *United States-Japan Trade Council Report,* No. 39, October 10, 1980.
4. See Shunzo Arai, *An Intersection of East and West, Japanese Business Management,* Kunio Odaka, *Japanese Management—A Forward Looking Analysis,* and S. Prakash Sethi et al, *The False Promise of the Japanese Miracle.*
5. Odaka, op. cit., pp. 65–6.
6. Arai, op. cit., p. 139.
7. "Japan's CEOs: How They View Their Jobs and Life," *Tokyo Business Today,* December 1991, pp. 58–63.
8. *Nikkei Weekly,* April 20, 1991.
9. According to a *Washington Post* survey, Japanese Diet members received annual salaries of $143,139 compared to $135,000 for U.S. Congressmen, $57,837 for German Bundestag members and $43,393 in the British House of Commons. *Washington Post,* February 5, 1991.
10. *The Economist,* August 10, 1991.
11. For more on the political system, see Karel van Wolferen, *The Enigma of Japanese Power,* and Jon Woronoff, *Politics, The Japanese Way.*
12. *Financial Times,* October 31, 1988.

6
Rich Nation, Poor People

Only Rich On Paper

Judging by most of the standard indicators, Japan has prospered over the years and become a highly affluent nation. It already accounts for 13 percent of world gross national product. That is second only to the United States and well ahead of any European country. It is also the world's biggest creditor. Per capita income reached $20,185 in 1990, placing it second only after the Swiss. Most people have cars, clothing, consumer gadgets, household appliances and sporting gear galore. More and more travel abroad or take vacations at home.

Surely, the economy has done nicely by them and there should be little reason to complain. Yet, when you look more closely, this supposed prosperity and affluence appear to be only surface phenomena. Deeper down, the Japanese are not faring so well and do not compare very favorably to others who are supposedly less endowed.

One elementary reason is that all of these comparative figures are in dollar terms. Having gone through several substantial appreciations of the yen, the latest doubling its value against the dollar, what the Japanese produce and earn is artificially bloated. So is what they buy in dollar terms. In yen terms, people are not doing much better than some years back and the upward slope is more gradual, with occasional dips.

Even more serious is that, as one Japanese economist pointed out, while the Japanese earn a lot, their money "does not go very far." Virtually everything is expensive. As we all know, housing is expensive, gas is expensive, and so are most utilities. Food can be incredibly pricey, with beef and rice six times international rates and most other foods multiples of foreign prices. Often enough articles produced in Japan may actually cost more than the same thing purchased abroad. Even more ludicrous, it is costlier to mail a letter from Tokyo to New York than New York to Tokyo, or make a call from Tokyo to London than London to Tokyo, or fly from Tokyo to Hong Kong than Hong Kong to Tokyo.

The purchasing power of the yen is, put quite frankly, appallingly limited. Without taking that into account, money remains a veil which makes Japan look more affluent than it really is. That has been shown by numerous studies, including a recent one by the thoroughly official Management and Co-ordination Agency. Using international statistics for 1990, it compared Japan's living standards to those in the United States, Europe and Asia. After correcting for what the yen can actually buy, Japan was placed much lower than before.

One of the major correctives was the average ratio of housing prices to average annual income, which was an unusually high 5.7 for Japan as a whole, and a forbidding 8.7 for Tokyo, compared to 4.6, 4.4 and 3.4 for Germany, Britain and the United States. Housing was such a burden that it left less room for other expenses. With about 25% of the budget going for food, compared to half that in the United States, there was not much left over for anything else.[1]

How then could the Japanese afford all the paraphernalia that clutters up their homes? Well, this time it is best to adjust for size, since they only have 25 square meters of living space per person compared to 61 square meters in the United States. Yet, in that reduced area, they crammed smaller TVs and VCRs, refrigerators that only hold a day's food, washing machines that run on cold water, and assorted miniaturized appliances. As for leisure, that was compressed into the limited free time and vacations granted them.

The biggest compression, however, is required for the biggest asset, one which almost boggles the mind . . . land. According to Deborah Allen of Claremont Economics Institute, "all the land in Japan is currently valued at over $13 trillion. This compares to $3.5 trillion for all the land in the United States, even though Japan has only 4 percent as much land as America."[2] But this extraordinary "wealth" does the ordinary Japanese little good. If he were to sell his land and still live in Japan, he would be forced to pay through the nose for new land. Only if he moved to the real world, somewhere outside of Japan, could he benefit. Within Japan, prices are almost meaningless as an indicator of value.

In reality, and this has been confirmed many times over, the Japanese are certainly no better off than most Europeans and Americans in purely material terms. When one adds leisure and quality of life, they are considerably worse off than most Westerners and even some Asians, like the Singaporeans whose income is a quarter as high. This much is increasingly realized by Japanese who travel and even those who stay home and view the outside world through the media.

That it is the Japanese who recognize they are not leading a very comfortable existence, and not just foreign critics or local intellectuals who say so, was shown by a survey conducted by Rengo, the largest labor union federation, in September 1990. The respondents were asked: Does the comfort level in your life befit Japan's powerful economic strength? The response was overwhelming. Only 4 percent answered "yes." Fully 83 percent responded "no."[3]

Should you be unconvinced by a survey from a trade union,

Which is worth more? The Emperor's backyard?
Or the state of California?

Credit: Foreign Press Center/Kyodo

even such a unanimous expression of dissatisfaction, you may care to see the results of a recent *Yomiuri Shimbun* poll. Although it was conducted in the midst of the 1990 boom, and 45 percent of the respondents conceded that the national economy was booming, 26 percent said they were worse off than the year before. More than 70 percent complained that prices were rising and, to make ends meet, 37 percent wanted a pay raise, 33 percent wanted pension reforms, 31 percent wanted tax cuts and 27 percent wanted increased controls on commodities prices. In keeping with our theme, the newspaper indicated that people are demanding ever more "to bridge the gap between national and individual wealth."[4]

Or you might be interested in the comments of a middle-class housewife reflecting on the situation of her friends.

"Where the household budget is concerned, they confess that they barely manage to make ends meet, these women in their comfortable-looking middle-class homes. I shudder to think what would happen to their families if the main breadwinner of the household were suddenly to fall ill or have an accident.

"Japan is hardly the wealthy nation it is made out to be. Its high per capita income is no more than a cruel statistical joke. From what my friends and acquaintances tell me, the average Japanese household runs on a tight budget indeed. Even the overseas vacations, the furs and the jewels that some indulge in are purchased on credit, which can be paid off with petty cash over the years. For the most part, we Japanese scrape by from day to day, never really getting ahead of the game until the day we die. Managing the family finances is a matter of rushing about patching up the holes as they appear."[5]

For such reasons, when the first version of this book was published, I coined the slogan of "rich nation, poor people." It sounds very noble, in the finest Meiji tradition. Yet, it could only be a goal pursued by fanatics or fools, since the normal goal should be rich nation, rich people. Nonetheless, the Japanese have created a perverse economic system in which very little real wealth is wrung out of absolutely staggering economic achievements.

The challenge is no longer to prove that the Japanese system has served the people quite poorly. That much is becoming obvious to even the most sycophantic. It is now necessary to understand why so much generates so little. That is the purpose of the following sections. One stresses another Woronoffian theme of an economy that is productive rather than fruitful. This is true especially in the manufacturing sector, the only one that is truly productive to begin with. Another cause is the gross inefficiency and waste of other sectors, already touched upon in the last chapter. There is also the astonishing freedom the authorities leave producers and distributors to fleece consumers, when they do not pitch in themselves.

Profitless Companies

One of the crucial explanations of why the Japanese do not have much to show for their considerable efforts is that the companies they work for do not seem to care much about profitability. In any ranking of business goals, profits come in toward the bottom, although they are uppermost for nearly all foreign companies. This means not only decadent Western ones but fledgling Asian firms. True, Japanese executives glibly talk about long-term profitability and the like. But that is turning into an exceedingly long term during which profits are quite modest.

It is obviously difficult to measure profitability exactly, no less compare it between countries. But the existing evidence is so conclusive and the gaps so large that it can be safely assumed that Japanese companies are among the most profitless in the world. For example, Iwao Nakatani, professor of economics at Hitotsubashi University, analyzed the top 1,000 international companies in the *Business Week* ranking. The average after-tax earnings of the Japanese contingent was only 2.4 percent. That compared with an international average of 4.6 percent and higher levels in the United States (5.6 percent), Germany (5.9 percent) and Great Britain (7.1 percent). In terms of return on capital, the performance of the Japanese companies was even more pitiful. They achieved an average rate of 8.6 percent compared with the world average of 15.1 percent and higher levels in Germany (13.7 percent), the United States (19.1 percent) and Great Britain (20.2 percent).[6]

These figures, it should be recalled, were for the biggest and best Japanese companies, the top performers. A broader study of 1,000 manufacturing firms by the Japan Development

Bank showed that their performance was not only lackluster but worsening over the years. The ratio of operating profit to sales peaked at 9.3 percent in 1969 and dropped to a low of 3.5 percent in the year to March 1987. Operating profits as a percentage of assets did much the same, peaking at 10 percent in 1969 and declining to 5 percent in fiscal 1987. If depreciation were added, the situation would have been even worse.[7] Yet, these were still fairly large companies in a reasonably bouyant manufacturing sector. If you take the corporate community as a whole, while perhaps somewhat exaggerated, it should be noted that over half of all companies have been declaring losses in recent years according to the tax administration.

Why is Japanese profitability low in absolute terms, low compared to other countries, and even low compared to the past? There are various reasons, some more noble or at least comprehensible than others.

One good reason, if "good" is an appropriate word, is that Japanese managers do not have to concentrate as much on profits as Western and other managers. They have relatively few shareholders which press for immediate returns, much of the stock being held by related companies, friendly banks, or the owners. Modest returns, comparable to those of other Japanese companies, has long been adequate in an economy where interest rates have been traditionally low. Moreover, by putting money to other purposes, other goals can be achieved such as expansion, diversification, stable employment, etc.

That may explain why managers have sought growth rather than profits and those who could boost sales a bit were rewarded more than those who could boost profits a bit. If, on the other hand, they lost sales or, worse, market share, they would be in deep trouble. In response to complaints about low profitability, they could respond that with larger turnovers and low profits they were doing as well as foreigners with smaller turnovers and higher profit rates. That was a fair answer, at least during the 1950s and 1960s when sales were growing swiftly. With sluggish sales growth during the 1970s and 1980s, it sounded more like a lame excuse.

Excuse or not, all Japanese managers were immersed in an incredibly competitive situation which bore no comparison with competition elsewhere and could properly be dubbed *kamikaze* competition. It was based on competition for market share. Unlike competition for profits, where the fact that your rivals make profits does not preclude your doing equally well, competition for market share is a clear win-lose battle. There are only 100 percent of market share and, if you gain a percent, somebody else must lose a percent. If that somebody else (or conceivably your own company) were to lose enough market share, it would completely disappear. With employees bound to their company, few alternative jobs and limited welfare, nobody could afford to lose and everybody had to fight on blindly no matter what the cost.

Competition for market share involved, first of all, an urge for expansion. The larger your capacity, the more you produced, the more product you could push and the cheaper the unit cost. If you could get ahead of the competitors, you could increase your share. However, if everybody expanded at the same time, the outcome would be excess capacity. That would have a very negative impact on profits. For one, companies would have spent too much on facilities that were too big, this hurting return on capital. Worse, with overcapacity, it was necessary to flog products at any price just to get rid of them.

That resulted in what the Japanese call *kato kyoso* or "excessive competition." Companies would not only forget profitability in an effort to gain market share and unload excess production, they would accept any necessary losses. After all, keeping the products was a pure loss and also implied inventory costs. There have been repeated bouts of *kato kyoso*

in the Japanese economy but some have gone down in hist[ory]
for their bitterness (if not folly). Worst was the battle betwe[en]
Honda and Yamaha to be number one for motorcycles. Also
memorable was the push by the VHC video-cassette recorder
team, led by Matsushita, to drive the Beta model, sponsored
by Sony, out of the market.

While one company or another may "win," if that is the
appropriate word, in the struggle for market share, this *kamikaze* competition hurts them all in certain ways. The most
visible is smaller profits or bigger losses. Equally significant
is that product cycles are getting ever shorter. The Japanese
appear surprised by this, as if it were an unfortunate accident.
It isn't. By insisting on improving on one another, and coming
out with new generations of articles in short order, they are
themselves contracting the cycle. And, every time a new
generation arrives, it stunts the older ones.

That happens for virtually everything, from TVs to autos,
but it is most visible for semiconductors. Over the years,
sales shot up and then collapsed for 4K chips, then 16K chips,
then 64K chips, then 1M chips. . . . Each time, companies
geared up, spent lavishly on equipment, expanded and over-produced. Prices fell due to excess supply and then dried up
further as the next generation appeared. Even the winners
admitted that. NEC's senior managing director, Hajime Sasaki, made a very quotable quote: "The way things are now,
no one will be able to make money from DRAMs."[8]

This was all compounded by certain Japanese "virtues,"
again an ambiguous word. There is no doubt that the Japanese
built mighty fine factories, with highly efficient machinery,
and scale economies. They often tore down older, but perfectly useable facilities, to put up greenfield plants that were
state-of-the-art. They refined their designs and improved their
quality. This was admirable and increased their competitiveness. But it was costing them a fortune! And it was absurd

when such expenses were required not only every ten or twenty years but with ever increasing frequency. No wonder the return on capital was so low.

The urge for expansion took Japanese companies in other directions as well. It was not enough to produce a narrow range of popular products. They always had to add to the range. For example, automakers insisted on producing not only middle-sized cars but smaller and larger ones, plus trucks, not only mid-priced cars but also luxury ones. In short, they tried to provide everything a client might want. So did the motorcycle makers. And producers of home appliances and consumer electronics generated thousands of different articles. Some of them were viable, others were not. After all, you cannot specialize in everything and be equally proficient at everything. But even the duds were kept for reasons of expansion and to avoid losing face.

Diversification was another form of expansion. If you had certain skills, trained personnel and enough capital, why not make something related to your field, say pharmaceuticals if you were in chemicals, or rigs if you were a shipbuilder? There might be some synergies involved. As elsewhere, however, the craze for diversification got out of hand. And it was intensified in Japan because, under lifetime employment, you were stuck with excess workers in many declining sectors. Thus, numerous companies set up subsidiaries just to house unwanted personnel.

At any rate, the Japanese went on an unbridled diversification spree in the 1980s. For example, the six biggest steelmakers created some 500 new ventures in just three years, including everything from fast food shops to semiconductors. Countless pharmaceutical, chemical, cosmetics, textile, foodstuff and even completely unrelated companies tried their hand at biotechnology. The outcome was mounting losses for most of the subsidiaries, some of which went bankrupt while others were secretly subsidized. While it occasionally increased sales, diversification was not much of a contribution to profits.

Two further drains must be mentioned, exporting and overseas investment. Exporting was a natural form of expansion, one much favored in an export-oriented economy in sectors where the Japanese did have superior products. But they rarely sold their products on the basis of inherent superiority. Instead, they were sold on price in order to increase market share more rapidly. The prices were so low on occasion as to be regarded as dumping, an allegation that was frequently proven. Whether dumping or not, exports were certainly subsidized by higher prices for the same goods or other goods sold locally by Japanese manufacturers. Since they were exported for less, quite naturally any profits were considerably smaller.

During the 1970s, and more intensively the 1980s, Japanese companies set up foreign ventures. Many of them were to manufacture goods offshore and avoid trade barriers and were thus not necessarily rational economic decisions. But even those that were suffered from the transplanting of *kamikaze* competition. Japanese rivals fought with one another, and local companies, for market share. They expanded production more than necessary and charged less than they could have gotten away with. Both strategies resulted in lower profits. In fact, MITI statistics showed that profits were only a few percent at best and many companies made losses.[9]

But that was less serious than another financial disaster that was periodically repeated. The Japanese were investing billions of dollars a year in overseas ventures, reaching a total of some $210 billion by 1990. A lot of that money was converted into weaker currencies, namely the dollar and dollar-related ones. Each time there was a depreciation of the dollar, the value was reduced in yen terms. Most recently, the Japanese lost half the value of their dollar-related investments, a mind-boggling figure that must have run into the tens of billions. No matter how long-term the Japanese thought, they would not make a penny out of many investments even over a period of decades.

Compared to these figures, one last act of profligacy may appear quite modest. It is no less significant, for it shows how Japanese business works. Year after year, Japanese companies have been spending a packet on entertainment, gifts and political donations. This exceeded ¥4 trillion in 1990, a level of ¥4 on every ¥1,000 of sales revenue, which few companies could afford. Yet, in Japan, it would be impossible to do business without luxurious wining and dining and gifts or other forms of "lubricant" to bureaucrats and politicians.[10]

Better late than never, by the 1990s it was dawning on the Japanese that profits were important. This started with academics like Iwao Nakatani, who wrote that "the exertion which results in minimal profitability through a low margin, high volume approach is really just a waste of time and effort."[11] Noritake Kobayashi of Keio Business School noticed a new thinking. "Let us forget about cutthroat free competition or so-called excessive competition and start to emphasize profit margin more than market share expansion."[12] Even Toyota, one of the worst culprits, finally decided that it would no longer formally set market share goals. But it will be hard to revamp the system as no company can afford to change alone since it would be crushed by the rest.

Pity The Poor Worker

It is very puzzling. Foreign observers who praise the Japanese management system, and seem to envy the Japanese worker, always overlook one little thing. Take this quote from Alan Blinder of Princeton. "Finance-dominated capitalism too often forgets that a business organization is made up of people and can function no better than they do. The Japanese rarely forget this. Indeed, Japanese managers commonly believe that the company's employees, not its machines, are its most important assets and are therefore to be valued, nurtured and—except in extremis—retained. So Japanese companies train their employees, see to their welfare, guarantee them job security, and offer career paths that blossom if the company flourishes."[13]

Wonderful. Assuming it is true. But, what about wages? What about the financial rewards of working for Japanese companies? Why is so little said about that? After all, even in Japan wages are important for workers. The reason may be that there is not much good to be said.

Obviously, it is not easy to compare wages from country to country. There are many variables, such as what should be included in terms of fringe benefits, bonuses, paid vacations, etc. Also, different categories of workers may have different wage levels, with some faring relatively well and others poorly. Still, no matter what the variables and what the yardsticks, it could hardly be claimed that Japanese workers are particularly well paid.

The most useful figures were compiled by the U.S. Labor Department for factory workers, the backbone of industrial economies, fairly comparable from place to place, and whose wages are crucial for competitiveness. In 1990, the average cost of an hour of labor (basic wages plus fringe benefits) was $12.64. That was slightly less than American workers and substantially less than workers in Germany and Sweden or even Italy and France.[14] Yet, as everybody knows, Japanese workers are driven harder and also, as we shall see, have much higher living costs.

Thus, while Japanese wage rates have been rising steadily since the war, and more rapidly in dollar terms due to the yen's appreciation, they have still not achieved Western standards. That can be explained by some of the points just elucidated, namely that companies have not earned large enough profits to pass more along to their employees and they have continued spending so much on equipment that less of whatever they had was left over for workers. Indeed, even if Japanese managers love workers more than machines, they rarely hesitate to buy more machinery whenever that can boost productivity while they always quibble over wages.

That may explain why, in the domestic context this time, Japanese wages are not especially generous. While they have admittedly been rising, it was not by very much. In most years, the improvement did keep ahead of inflation. But that was inflation as measured by government statistics, and which did not take adequate account of mounting housing and other expenses. Consequently, many workers were really not keeping up and, in order to pay the bills, more men were taking second jobs while more wives entered the labor force and both did overtime.

Less auspiciously, real wages did not keep up with labor productivity. This means workers did not share equally with the company any benefits gained by the increased efficiency of using machinery, machinery which often reduced the number of jobs available. More broadly, as a Marxist economist explained, "labor's relative share (of economic growth) in Japan has been much lower than that in other industrial countries and the long-term trend has been to keep it low."[15] But this is not only a Marxist or Socialist complaint. Sony's Akio Morita conceded the point and it was confirmed by the statistics of the International Labour Organisation.

That was not the only way in which workers were squeezed. Some of the other manifestations are so cheap and petty that one can only wonder why management insists. For example, sick pay is only 60 percent of normal pay, which explains why many employees either work when they are ill or take off vacation days to visit the doctor. Overtime is only paid at 125 percent of normal wages, not time-and-a-half or double-time, according to circumstances, as in the West. By the way, that only applies to official overtime. Extra hours spent achieving a quota are usually contributed "voluntarily." And managers are not paid for overtime, no matter how long.

This is further imbedded in a support system that is very rudimentary and iffy. The minimum wage is so minimal as to be meaningless, usually set at a level much lower than going wages. But even it can be evaded in the case of home-workers who are paid by the piece. Unemployment coverage only lasts six months, much less than in the West. Moreover, it is extremely hard to get. Most beneficiaries belong to larger companies and are often undergoing retraining, which is not really unemployment. It can rarely be obtained by those in more tenuous positions, like temporary workers or part-timers, and homeworkers never benefit because officially they are not employed and therefore cannot become unemployed. The self-employed, a very large category in Japan, are also excluded.

Social security and company pensions are rather skimpy for all but regular workers. Employers can avoid obligations toward temporary workers by constantly renewing short-term contracts or hiring them through temp agencies. Part-timers are even worse off. Homeworkers again have nothing. As for the frills, they are sadly lacking. Maternity leave and provision for childcare were minimal and often shirked by adroitly ridding the company of women once they married or approached childbirth and then hiring them back once the children were grown.

These are hardly signs of a caring society. And, like it or not, Japanese tradition does not lay much emphasis on looking after one another, especially if that implies looking after out-siders. But the real culprit was again competition. Managers firmly believed they could not survive unless they were the fittest and therefore, among other things, dumped young mar-ried women or refused to hire the handicapped. They also felt they had to invest in more machinery to keep up with local competitors and to pare labor costs to compete with foreign rivals, some of which employed very cheap labor.

Regularly, year after year, the Japan Federation of Employers Associations (Nikkeiren) adopted an aggressive stance on wage hikes. It steadfastly insisted that they not exceed inflation or productivity growth, whichever was lower, and sometimes pleaded extraordinary circumstances to keep them from rising even that much. It also militated against expanded unemployment coverage, excessive (i.e. Western-style) social security and other frills. And it managed to hold the line.

Regularly, year after year, the Japanese trade unions organized a "spring offensive" (*shunto*) during which wage demands were submitted to management and workers agitated for improvement. Alas, much of this was a charade, and management knew it. Union membership, while high (about 25 percent) was steadily declining and union members were divided among thousands of unions, usually on a company or factory basis. This allowed managers to play them off against one another. In the end, the *shunto* wage demands were never met and, as noted, wages failed to keep up adequately.[16]

This was a nasty fact of life for workers, who were perfectly aware of their position. Complaints came not only from the trade unions or Communist and Socialist parties, workers sent letters to the editor and responded testily to public opinion polls. One was particularly interesting, since it compared workers in such varied countries as Australia, Great Britain, Germany and the United States. Two out of three Japanese workers complained that they were underpaid, an unusually high level. Only 31 percent were satisfied with their fringe benefits, an unusually low level. They were also negative about working relationships, supervision and management.[17]

Given the relationship between management and labor, and solid government backing of management, it is not likely that the situation will change. The only hope, a rather flimsy one, is that foreign countries and trade unions will exert pressure to boost Japanese wages (and make Japan less competitive). But Japan, Inc. would never stand for that, despite its supposed affection for people.

Let The Consumer Pay

One of the reasons why ordinary Japanese got so little out of the economic progress is that, as noted, prices are higher than elsewhere. This view was once energetically disputed by the Japanese government. But a recent U.S.-Japan joint study within the Structural Impediments Initiative proved that point conclusively. Among the findings were that the same German spark plug was four times more expensive in Japan, British jam was more than twice as expensive, and even a bottle of Japanese *sake* cost 44 percent more in Japan than the United States.[18] These results can be borne out by anyone who has shopped in Japan and America or Europe and knows how costly things are.

Still, this joint study should be considered even more closely, without overemphasizing the more conspicuous differences. Of the 112 products surveyed, fully 67 percent were more expensive in Japan. This included not only American products sold in Japan but Japanese products sold in Japan, almost a third of which cost more at home than abroad. To rule out the possibility that this was explained by normal costs of importing, the prices of products from third countries sold in both America and Japan were studied. Nearly all of those were more expensive in Japan. Nor were the discrepancies minor. The average price was 37 percent higher in Japan, a substantial levy on the consumer.

There are various explanations for such high prices, two crucial ones being related to the excessive emphasis on exporting. As mentioned, due to an exaggerated urge for market share abroad, Japanese companies frequently inflated the domestic price in order to subsidize exports. This means that Jap-

Can you imagine what it was like before
the distribution "revolution?"

Credit: JNTO

anese consumers have to pay more than otherwise and quite
often more than foreign consumers, especially for whatever
products are being targeted at the time. Obviously, Japanese
makers could not keep their prices artificially high if foreign
imports were cheaper. That problem is avoided by keeping
foreign imports out of the market or restricted to niches. The
only prices at which the average Japanese can buy are the local
ones even if they know the products are cheaper abroad.

Of course, not all foreign products can be blocked or marginalized. So, the second best solution is to make them as expensive in Japan as Japanese products, even if they were
considerably cheaper back home. The easiest way of doing

this is to keep them out of the mass merchandisers, many of which are controled by Japanese companies, and relegate them to smaller shops and boutiques that specialize in foreign goods. Many of these goods, by the way, are sold as *haku-raihin* or "foreign luxuries," where price is hardly a consideration and a higher price actually adds to the product's appeal.

There are other techniques as well. One is to limit the sources of supply so that those which sell the product can safely raise prices. That occurs for imported beef, which must pass through certain distributors, who actually sell to one another and swell the price to nearly the level of domestic beef before it reaches the consumer. Another occurs for imported goods where the importer has an exclusive contract and can charge whatever the market will bear. For gasoline, a much more widely used item, the various gas stations tend to charge a standard price, one proposed by the refiners. And the refiners can keep that price high (several times higher than abroad) because MITI prohibits parallel imports.

Just how effective the distributors, in collusion with the manufacturers, can be in keeping the costs of imports up was demonstrated most convincingly each time there was an appreciation of the yen. By definition, if the value of the yen rises against the dollar, products priced in dollars should automatically become cheaper. They should actually become considerably cheaper given the major currency adjustments in the early 1970s and mid-1980s. Yet, each time, import prices only declined slightly, if at all. That was noticed by the consumers, media and even government. But the distributors managed to hold on to huge unjustified profits.

How can the distributors get away with it? That is quite simple. Manufacturers often control distributors directly or indirectly. These shops, which often only handle one brand, are asked to sell at the official retail price, one which guarantees a profit all around, but keeps prices high. Not only that, they are discouraged from discounting, even in hard times, to move products. They are also forbidden from selling to third parties which might discount. So there really is only one price and the consumer has to pay it whether he likes it or not.

Admittedly, in recent years, there has been a trend toward supposedly "independent" retailers which carry articles from various manufacturers. However, since the makers tend to align their prices with one another, this only means that consumers can buy similar products at similar prices, hardly an advantage. And there are few real bargains since even the "discounters" tend to charge generally acceptable prices within a merchant community that colludes informally. The fact that retail price maintenance and price fixing, the two keys to this phenomenon, are strictly illegal has not prevented them from becoming very widespread. So there really is not much price competition and the consumer has to pay up.

In some instances, this relatively informal price fixing goes even further. Actual cartels are formed to set and maintain the prices of specific articles. Many of them, hundreds in fact, have been established formally and legally by the Ministry of International Trade and Industry in order to help ailing industries. But others helped themselves by creating illegal cartels. There may have been thousands of those, who knows?, since most avoid detection. Among those which have been caught by the Fair Trade Commission were cartels for cement, packing material, cleaning equipment, pharmaceuticals, etc. [19]

In these cases, the cartels and practices are patently illegal and the FTC is expected to take action. Since it is basically an emanation of MITI, it rarely does unless prodded by foreign criticism and pressure. Thus, just a small share of the infractions resulted in legal action and rather few participants were fined. Even the fines were paltry and hardly enough to inhibit the practice. Companies were just obliged to pay from 0.5–2 percent of their illicit gains and could keep the rest.

Increasing the rate to 6 percent, still much lower than in other advanced countries, is unlikely to prove much more effective.

To make it short and bitter, prices are not high just because Japan is a small island nation, with a multi-layered distribution system, and high labor costs, as some defenders claim. Consumers are clearly being ripped off by distributors, sometimes through gentle collusion, often enough through illegal practices. This continues because nothing much is done by the authorities, including supposed "watchdogs." So much for the Japanese consumer being "God." In the West, even the devil would get a better deal.

The situation would probably improve if there were enough criticism from those being fleeced, namely the consumers. Alas, there is no strong reaction. They do grumble about high prices and the difficulty in making ends meet. They do realize that many things are cheaper aboard than at home. They come back from overseas trips loaded down with purchases. That, however, is the extent of the effort. They have not banded together in consumer movements that have any notable political clout. Some do exist in name, including several with a large membership and long history, but their efforts are feeble and most often futile.

Worse, Japanese consumers—especially young women—are moving in the wrong direction. They remain sticklers for quality and service but forget the price factor. They do not engage in enough comparison shopping, nor do they read many consumer magazines, and instead let themselves be guided by fashions and brand names. Thus, according to a *Nihon Keizai Shimbun* survey, consumers simply assumed that expensive clothing would last longer and higher priced products would be safer. This, according to the analysts, "revealed the rather blind faith that many Japanese have in high prices and name brands as automatic guarantees of safety and quality."[20]

The distributors have certainly noticed this. There are more exclusive boutiques than ever and department stores only carry expensive goods. The producers have also noticed this. In another comparative study by MITI, American businesses listed low price as the second most important factor in competitiveness. For Japanese companies, it was only number six.[21] And the government realizes that cheaper prices do not have a high enough priority to bother. So, Japanese consumers will continue paying through the nose for many years to come. Perhaps they deserve it.

Government-Induced Waste

One other noteworthy source of wastefulness and price gouging which considerably reduced the wealth of the average individual was government meddling. This may come as a surprise to some readers because Japan is so widely praised for its industrial policy and targeting of industries which became world-class. But that is only part of the picture. In many sectors, there was no targeting. In yet others, there was inexcusable protection and sloth. Even where competition did reign, and the more efficient prevailed, that was often more an outcome of foreign pressure than government initiative.

Taking a brief look back, in the 1950s and 1960s, most Japanese industries were protected by quotas, tariffs and other barriers which kept out the then highly competitive goods of American or European rivals. It was only after the quotas and tariffs were forcibly dismantled, under pressure from foreign trading partners, that MITI got serious about targeting so that local companies could resist the onslaught. Even then, it retained nontariff barriers to shelter producers and otherwise allowed them to create further obstacles in the distribution system.

The Ministry of International Trade and Industry certainly played a constructive role in rationalizing and strengthening sectors like steel, computers, machinery and so on. But others emerged more or less on their own, including automobiles, consumer electronics and motorcycles. And several were encouraged by other ministries, like shipbuilding through the Ministry of Transport, telecommunications through the Ministry of Post and Telecommunications and pharmaceuticals through the Ministry of Health. That was the positive face of targeting.

The negative side, less often mentioned, is that each of these sectors benefited from costly support, not only subsidies and R&D projects but protection which made their products artifically expensive. Worse, when some of them went into decline (often after phases of overexpansion), they were supported and protected even more, although they contributed little to the economy. Such sectors included shipbuilding and shipping, petrochemicals, textiles, etc. This sort of assistance, as everywhere else, had more costs than benefits for the general public.

Other sectors were also supported and protected excessively and at great cost to the consumers and taxpayers. Some came under the Ministry of Transport, namely the airlines, shipping lines and railways. The state monopoly Japan National Railways was uncommonly prodigal, run more sloppily than the private lines and spending ever more money on the *shinkansen* which were exceedingly costly and duplicated old lines. The international carrier JAL, and the domestic carriers ANA and TDA, were not only protected from foreign competition, they arranged domestic flights at their convenience. This allowed them to charge excessive rates on planes that were frequently packed.

In telecommunications, under the Ministry of Post and Telecommunications, fees were unpardonably high because there was *no* competition during most of the postwar period. Nippon Telegraph and Telephone and Kokusai Denshin Denwa could charge virtually anything they wanted as long as it was authorized by the Diet, which usually happened.

They must have been inherently uncompetitive because Japan's telephone, telegraph and other services were lagging for more modern systems, from mobile phones to VANs. Indeed, no sooner had state-run NTT been privatized than it discovered it could not even ward of its tiny adversaries and make a decent profit.

One of the worst, yet most essential, sectors was finance. On the one hand, financial institutions were allowed to charge individuals exorbitant rates for most of their services. This included insurance coverage, bank transfers and other operations, brokerage commissions, and so on. On the other, they offered less than many foreign counterparts. Most noticeable were the low interest rates prevailing for savings accounts. But even they were preferable to the mediocre returns, and high risk, of the investment trusts.

That is because the Ministry of Finance kept the sector closed and regulated much longer than manufacturing and still controls it informally today. Liberalization only came in the 1970s and deregulation, partial at least, in the 1980s. But there is still hardly any competition to speak of. Instead, what has reigned is the "convoy system" whereby rates were set at levels that enabled even the weakest bank, insurance company, securities firm, etc. to keep afloat. This obviously encouraged inefficiency, since the rest only had to do somewhat better than the slowest, worst performer in the convoy to make money. Consumers lost twice, once due to higher rates, the second time due to inexcusable inefficiency.

Since the financial intermediaries knew they would be covered by bureaucrats who took pride in allowing no institution to fail, they took greater risks than they should and ran up bigger losses on occasion. They eagerly loaned too much to real estate companies and land speculators, often on insufficient collateral, during the various speculative binges. They also backed stock speculators, some of whom pulled out too late. At the behest of MOF itself, they bought U.S. dollar bonds, many of whose value was halved during the latest dollar devaluation. Sure enough, when the bubbles burst in the early 1990s, they were bailed out and the burden for foolish lending was shifted to the public.

For agriculture, there never was much benefit and costs have been crushing, more than in any other country which supported and protected its farm sector. They were nearly twice that of the European Community, which was also plagued by small farms and high costs.[22] Not even the Europeans would have accepted policies that made the staple crop, rice, six times as expensive as abroad, and everything else dear as well. That is only part of the cost, i.e. what is paid by the consumers. When you add the taxes levied to finance the operation, the amounts were even greater. The total bill probably added up to Y10 trillion or more a year by the early 1990s.

While the multi-layered distribution system is blamed for part of the high cost of goods, and rightly so, it should not be forgotten that official policy contributed. For it was the government that adopted laws, and the bureaucrats who invented regulations, to slow down the introduction of large-scale stores. This delayed a process that was clearly in the interest of consumers and would have permitted considerable savings. In the construction sector, other absurd laws and regulations added to the cost of housing. This included measures protecting "farm" land, others preventing the construction of high-rise apartment buildings, and one allowing neighbors to block the erection of structures that deprived them of their sunlight even notionally.

One last muck-up should be mentioned, not only because it was symbolic but because it occurred in a sector one assumed Japan would excel in. In 1969, the Nuclear Ship Development Agency launched a nuclear-powered ship called the Mutsu. Already on its maiden voyage, the reactor developed a radioactive leak. Even after the repair work, which was unaccountably slow, no port was willing to accept the ship which was regarded as unsafe (unless, of course, the government sweetened the offer). Finally, after wandering about for two decades and accomplishing nothing more than making the government look foolish, the ship was decommissioned. The final bill was ¥100 billion, many times higher than the original estimate of ¥14 billion.

Most of this wastefulness, inefficiency and resulting high costs can be traced to the bureaucrats who, as we all now know, run the ministries. But the politicians contributed in their way. They imposed high prices for rice, to gather the farm vote, and introduced laws to protect small retailers, to collect their vote. They were also the ones who insisted on adding more railway lines and stations, whether they were needed or not, because that guaranteed elections. Then, to cover the costs, they had JNR subsidized. Friends of NTT, KDD and JAL also saw to it that they were supported.

Japan's politicians also had a taste for monumental, showcase construction projects, even while neglecting more ordinary facilities that were urgently needed. One of these was the Seikan Tunnel, the world's longest tunnel, which was unfortunately built at the wrong time, in the wrong place, and never put to good use. Another was a huge bridge to Shikoku, with a toll so costly that many commuters could not afford to take it and used the ferry. There was also Tokyo's international airport at Narita, supposedly built to relieve pressure on an older airport that could have been expanded at half the cost. Alas, due to quarrels with local farmers and allied radicals, only one runway was opened and that at an extraordinary expense. This saddled Japan with three of the world's prize "white elephants," not the sort of thing you would expect.

But they should have company since national and local politicians are busily nurturing more. Work is beginning on the world's longest suspension bridge, there should a tunnel-highway and bridge linking Tokyo and Chiba, and a dozen new airports. Meanwhile, the international airport near Osaka is running into trouble. Most serious is that the artificial island it is being erected on is slowly sinking into the bay. Thus, the airport cannot be finished on time and should cost far more than foreseen. Not really fazed, Osaka is working on an "intelligent city" and a Techno-Port, the supposed "project of the century." And there is no shortage of futuristic plans for the 21st century, if the taxpayers can afford it.

Admittedly, protecting business and building public works are legitimate functions of politicians, even if they may be economically counterproductive. Bid-rigging is not. Yet, as repeated scandals have shown, *dango* or pre-arranged bidding among contractors is widespread. And some of the extra money they siphon off is given to politicians and bureaucrats who helped them as bribes, kickbacks or more innocuously campaign funds and wining and dining.[23] Just how much money that adds to the public works bill is uncertain, yet even 10–15 percent on the hundreds of trillions of yen spent on government projects implies losses of tens of trillions over the years.[24]

NOTES

1. *Yomiuri*, January 4, 1991.
2. *Business Tokyo*, October 1991, p. 12.
3. *Productivity in Japan*, Spring 1991, p. 6.
4. *Yomiuri*, February 12, 1990.
5. Seiko Tanabe, "Prodigal Children, Impoverished Parents," *Japan Echo*, Vol. XVII, 1990, p. 61.
6. *Nikkei Weekly*, October 19, 1991.
7. *Far Eastern Economic Review*, August 10, 1989, p. 50.
8. *Nikkei Weekly*, July 27, 1991.
9. MITI, *Overseas Activities of Japanese Business Enterprises*, annual.
10. See Annual Reports of the National Tax Administration Agency.
11. *Nikkei Weekly*, October 19, 1991.

126

12. *Tokyo Business Today*, February 1991, p. 43.
13. *Business Week*, November 11, 1991, p. 22.
14. Other hourly rates were $14.77 in the United States, $21.53 in Germany, $20.93 in Sweden, $16.41 in Italy and $15.23 in France. *Wall Street Journal*, January 6, 1992.
15. Shigeyoshi Tokunaga, "A Marxist Interpretation of Japanese Industrial Relations," in Taishiro Shirai (ed.), *Contemporary Industrial Relations in Japan*, p. 318. See also Takura Seiyama, "Radical Interpretation of Policies," and Toshio Kurokawa, "Problems of the Working Class," in T. Morris-Suzuki, *Japanese Capitalism Since 1945*.
16. See Hirosuke Kawanishi, *Enterprise Unionism in Japan*.
17. *Wall Street Journal*, November 13, 1991.
18. *Financial Times*, May 21, 1991.
19. See the Annual Reports of the Fair Trade Commission.
20. *Keizai Weekly*, March 16, 1991.
21. *Productivity in Japan*, Summer 1990, p. 3.
22. *The Economist*, June 8, 1991.
23. See William J. Holstein, *The Japanese Power Game*, Karel van Wolferen, *The Enigma of Japanese Power*, and Jon Woronoff, *Politics, The Japanese Way*.
24. See Ellis S. Krauss and Isobel Coles, "Built-in Impediments: The Political Economy of the U.S.-Japan Construction Dispute," in Kozo Yamamura (ed.), *Japan's Economic Structure: Should It Change?*, pp, 333–58.

7
What Quality Of Life?

Of Rabbit Hutches . . .

If the Japanese are doing poorly with regard to monetary rewards, once adjusted to the purchasing power of the yen, they are doing even worse for quality of life. It is widely known, and statistically verifiable, that the Japanese live in pretty cramped housing, with rather mediocre amenities, and have precious little leisure. They are not quite "workaholics living in rabbit hutches," as it was once put, but they are also not enjoying a quality of life comparable to that of other advanced, and many less developed, societies.

Of course, the friends of Japan will complain that quality of life is a concept that does not travel. Maybe the Japanese like living cheek by jowl in tight quarters, maybe they are happiest when they are toiling, maybe they derive great pleasure from sacrificing for their company, and so on. Bill Emmott even went so far as to argue that, all things considered, "life in Japan is not so bad after all."[1] The fatal flaw in this view, alas, is that it is not shared by the Japanese. As we shall see, every official survey and every personal conversation will show that the Japanese are not really happy with their quality of life, however it may be defined. Still, it is helpful to transpose the concept . . . especially when the results remain the same.

For the 1989 White Paper on Livelihood, the Economic Planning Agency polled Japanese men and women to see whether they enjoyed *yutori*. It can be defined narrowly as "freedom," "ease," or the "good life." But it connotes much more. It is an intangible quality that expresses a sense of contentment. While *yutori* was obviously something that most Japanese sought, according to the poll less than half the men and somewhat more women attained it. The problem was not so much economic conditions, which had improved, but a lack of free time and spiritual fulfillment.[2]

Causes of inadequate *yutori* abound. The most visible derive from the physical living conditions. That Japanese housing is inferior to the West is clear enough. According to figures from the Management and Coordination Agency, the living space per person was a scanty 25 square meters compared to an ample 61 square meters in the United States. Europeans admittedly had less room than Americans, but they were not hemmed in as much as the Japanese. Indeed, even the Koreans had more living space.[3]

This was only part of the problem. Japanese homes, in addition to being small and crowded, were often quite ugly. Many were ramshackle wooden crates or forbidding concrete blocks with a minimum of decoration, and poorly kept up at that. Hastily thrown together, most would not have met building regulations or quality standards abroad, and they would be sadly run-down in a decade or two. Few had central heating or air-conditioning and the plumbing was not the best. Surrounding them might be a patch of greenery used as a scrawny "garden" or a parking place. The only touch of class was often a ridiculously high-sounding name.

Nonetheless, this second-rate and sometimes third-rate housing was selling for prices that the finest mansions and condos could not command in the outside world. Even after the price rise slackened, the average cost of an apartment in Tokyo was ¥100 million. A really nice house by Japanese standards, but no big deal by foreign ones, could easily run into ¥500 million. Something even foreigners would regard as grand might cost ¥2 billion.

These are not only prices that made foreigners' eyes pop, they made Japanese spirits sink. Families had to set aside ever more money to buy a home and then pay off the mortgage. Mortgage fees frequently absorbed 20–40 percent of the family's monthly income and increasingly, to meet them, payments had to be stretched out over two generations. That assumed that a home was at all affordable. By 1990, according to the Management and Coordination Agency, the ratio of average housing prices to average annual income was 5.7 for Japan as a whole and 8.7 in Tokyo.[4] Unfortunately, it was generally felt that the most a family could afford to pay was five years' wages.

Obviously, more and more Japanese simply cannot afford a home. That is a painful blow to quality of life and *yutori*. For owning a home is not only a question of having more comfortable living quarters but also a source of security. With a home, one is more stable, a better credit risk, a solid member of society and a possessor of property that could be mortgaged or sold in old age. With home ownership an official government goal and a personal dream, this increasing inability marked a watershed in Japanese society and created a substantial class of have-nots.

In order to get a home, or a condo, or quite simply any place to live, Japanese employees and workers have had to forage ever further afield. This meant that an increasing share, especially in the big cities, live an hour, two or even three from their place of work. That implies two, four or six hours commuting time a day. This is done in dreary trains and buses, often requiring several transfers plus a walk each way. Commuting is not only time-consuming, it is expensive and

"Rabbit hutches" may be an understatement.

it is exhausting when trains and buses are packed to several times official capacity.

The homes many Japanese live in are not even parts of "neighborhoods" in any real sense. They are built helter-skelter, wherever land is available and affordable, often one by one. There is little town planning, so residential zones rarely exist and you may be living next door to merchants and tradesmen or, quite possibly, restaurants, golf ranges, *karaoke* joints and even factories. There is occasionally no recognizable town center, one where people would tend to congregate and around which a community spirit might develop. Anyway, with such long commuting times and limited leisure, most of the male inhabitants of the bedroom suburbs are away.

Amenities, as is now widely known, are lacking. Here are just a few examples. Only 41 percent of the Japanese have mains drains, compared to 95 percent in Britain and 73 percent in America. Only 60 percent have flush toilets. Only 20 percent of the electric cables are buried underneath the streets, the rest draped on ugly poles.[5] There are few parks and gardens for adults or playgrounds for children. There is also a marked lack of cultural facilities, concert halls, theaters, museums, etc. More embarrassing, Japanese schools are rather shoddy affairs as concerns their physical appearance, crowded classrooms, crummy equipment and scruffy playing fields.

Still, if there is one failure that appears both inexplicable and absurd, it is the shortage of roads and highways. Japanese companies make cars, the government promotes car ownership and there are 60 million vehicles in the country. But there is inadequate parking space so that many owners must pay for expensive and distant lots. The roads they use are often unpaved. And many of them do not even have sidewalks where pedestrians are safe. Presently, there are only 5 meters of road per car compared to six times that in France or the United States. No wonder the roads are always packed, traffic moves at a snail's pace and there are hour-long traffic jams on the misnamed expressways.

What is particularly worrisome about all this is that the

situation has scarcely improved despite countless promises from the government, more often to foreign countries than the Japanese people. The size of the average home has only increased marginally over the years although the government sets goals and minimums (which are never met). It also adopts enormous budgets to build more amenities and cultural facilities. Yet, no matter how much money is allocated, it is never enough to keep up with needs and assuredly not enough to endow Japan with an infrastructure that is almost taken for granted elsewhere.

Will things improve during the 1990s and into the 21st century, which the government is painting as a period of fulfillment? That is hardly likely. For the constant rise in the cost of land has already doomed many indispensable projects. For some, there will not be big enough plots, or plots suitably located, or plots that the owners will sell. For all of them, the cost of land will be so high that little will remain for the building and equipment. Already by now, land costs absorb as much as 90 percent of the total budget of many public works. No matter how much money is allocated, it will not be enough!

And Workaholics

The other, no longer very complimentary, description of the Japanese which is increasingly accepted abroad—and at home—is a nation of "workaholics." As was made abundantly clear in earlier sections, this may apply more to hours than content of work. Still, for the former, it is certainly apt. According to Ministry of Labor statistics, the average Japanese worker spent 2,159 hours on the job in 1990. While this was admittedly somewhat less than in developing Asian countries, it was substantially more than in advanced Western ones with which Japan liked to compare itself. The gap amounted to almost 200 hours more than in the United States and 400 hours more than in France and Germany.

What is interesting to note about this long schedule is that it has hardly improved for quite some time. True, it is somewhat less than last year and the year before, a point the government prides itself on. But the Japanese were actually putting in fewer hours in the late 1970s than the 1980s and even today. So, the trends have not been consistently in the right direction. If anything, they moved in undesired ways. For, while regular working hours decreased, overtime kept on growing. What workers gained formally, they more than lost informally.

Moreover, given the crucial role of overtime, it should be stressed that the statistics only include official overtime that has been clocked in. Many more hours are contributed more or less "voluntarily." As noted, employees tend to come early, leave late and shorten lunch and other breaks. This can easily add up to another hour a day and 200 hours a year. In factories, workers are kept on to "finish the work" or engage in QC and other activities, often unpaid. Salarymen and especially managers are expected to put in extra time, also frequently without pay and without being recorded. Under such conditions, official statistics significantly understate the work load.

They also do not include other items which are more borderline, like socializing with co-workers, clients or suppliers. Most employees, at all levels, are expected to go for a drink with the boys (or girls) after work. It is part of their job to have a friendly drink with counterparts in other companies with which they do business. To call this a mixture of business and pleasure as opposed to business as usual would be obliging, but incorrect. Yet, these after-hours chores can absorb hundreds of hours a year for many.

Naturally, if hours devoted to work are long, those given

over to relaxation are short. The average Japanese receives some fifteen days of paid vacation, more or less in line with American levels if considerably shorter than European. But the average Japanese does not even take the full allotment. Most claimed only half recently, and very rarely at a go. Holidays of more than a week are quite rare except among women. On occasion, even the Saturday off is returned to the company to accomplish a particularly pressing task or play golf with other managers or clients.

Why do the Japanese work so long? Is it because they really enjoy working, that they are "workaholics" in the true sense? Is it because they really love their company? Is it even because they are bucking for promotion? Not according to those concerned. When asked why they worked so long, 44 percent of a *Yomiuri Shimbun* poll said they could not maintain their standard of living without doing overtime and 43 percent said they could not finish their work within regular working hours.[6] As for giving back vacation days, according to another poll, the main reasons were that workers did not want to cause trouble with their colleagues or give the boss a bad impression.[7]

It is perfectly evident that the Japanese do not want to work such long hours. What is even more extraordinary, considering that many need the extra money, is that most would gladly accept a tradeoff of less work for less money. According to the Public Opinion Survey on the Life of the Nation by the Prime Minister's Office, for years already less than a quarter of the respondents said they would sacrifice free time for more income while more than half, or twice as many, said they would not cut back on free time to increase their income. This same survey, and many others, repeatedly showed that one of the highest priorities of the Japanese was more free time.[8] And "leisure" has been a popular theme ever since the 1970s.

Unfortunately, the Japanese have not been getting what

Main Priorities in Life

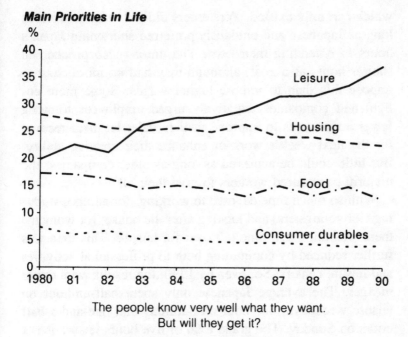

The people know very well what they want.
But will they get it?

Source: Prime Minister's Office, *Public Opinion Survey
on the Life of the Nation*, 1990.

they want, this despite official measures by the government.
First came the decision to impose the five-day week. Although
that could be achieved by granting as little as one weekend
a month, there are still many companies with a predominantly
six-day week and relatively few with every weekend off. Then
came the switch from a legal 48-hour week to a 44-hour
week. And, just to play it safe, special holidays were proclaimed, like Sports, Culture and Respect-For-The-Aged
Days. Still, as the statistics show, the number of hours worked
remained exceptionally high.

It was obvious that nothing could be accomplished until
the companies decided it was also in their best interest. To
help them along, the government cited foreign pressure,

which certainly existed. Westerners did not want to work as long as Japanese and obviously preferred shortening Japan's hours to extending their own. The unions also proclaimed shorter hours as a goal, although they had no more clout to impose this than to impose higher wages. Some more enlightened companies tentatively urged employees to work fewer hours so as to improve their morale, let them recover for the next week's work or enhance their creative ability. But little could be achieved as long as other companies, the majority, pressured workers to give their all.

With so much time devoted to working (for adults), studying (for youngsters) and looking after the house (for women), there was not much time left over for leisure. This time was further reduced by commuting both to professional activities and leisure centers. So, even by 1990, the results were rather meager. The average Japanese only spent half-an-hour on leisure weekdays, one hour on Saturday and one-and-a-half hours on Sunday. The grand total of five hours leisure is not very much.[9] But it is at least more than the pitiful two hours a week in the 1970s. And that is what has generated a so-called "leisure boom."

Over the years, there is no doubt that the Japanese have engaged in more leisure pursuits. These run a wide gamut but, alas, most are quite passive. There is much watching of television, playing of videos, listening to music and puttering around the garden. More vigorous activities, like sports, are done less frequently, and often in a modified form. Thus, many of the nation's 17 million golfers only play once or twice a month, and that in a cage of sorts rather than on a green. Many of the 15 million fishermen never get near a stream, they practice in local "ponds" constructed for the purpose and regularly stocked with inedible fish.

More significant is that the growth in leisure has been very lopsided. The ordinary salarymen or factory workers, your hard-core "workaholic," still do not do much. In fact, most

of them just nap or while the time away. The biggest prac-
titioners are students, young working women, housewives
whose children have grown up and retirees. They put in the
bulk of the leisure and most frequently travel locally or
abroad.

Thus, despite any progress, there is a lot more to be
achieved in terms of ordinary leisure. Not only must the
leisure time be extended and the leisure facilities expanded
so that more can participate at reasonable costs, it is necessary
to teach whole classes of Japanese what leisure is all about
so that they may partake intelligently and profitably rather
than just wasting time.

Spiritual Want

There is another, extremely significant, but terribly elusive
aspect of the quality of life and *yutori*. It can perhaps best
be summed up as "spiritual fulfillment." It is hard to define
just what this means since it varies from person to person
and country to country. Still, some aspects are reasonably
obvious and have already been confirmed by the Japanese as
important to them. Moreover, over the years, the Japanese
have markedly shifted their priority from material prosperity
to personal happiness.[10] Alas, given the long hours, inadequate funds and facilities, and the invasiveness of the company and society, that goal has not been easy to achieve.

This can most readily be shown for the family, which still
rates very high for most Japanese. In fact, in the latest Public
Opinion Survey on the Life of the Nation, nearly 90 percent
of the respondents said they found fulfillment with their families, well ahead of any other source. Yet, it is absolutely
clear that there is a growing crisis in the family. There are
ever more nuclear families and fewer extended families,
which is a normal concomitant of modernization and urbanization. Meanwhile, the average family is getting ever

smaller as fewer children are begot. And women (and perforce men) are marrying at later ages, if at all. More serious is the increase in divorces, single-parent families and aged living alone.

Part of this can be traced to purely physical causes, one decisive factor being small dwellings which make it hard for too many to live together. The lack of money also plays a role, with ever more women working, and working for longer periods, with less time to look after the children. There is equally a tendency for young women to enjoy the "good life," namely the material comfort of a salary without having to look after a husband or kids, quite demanding responsibilities in Japan.

But even duly constituted families are going through a very rough patch. As noted, the father has to work long hours and spend more time commuting. This keeps many men away from the family too much. They leave for work before the kids are up, they return after the kids have gone to sleep or at least too late to have dinner with them. They are not even available on weekends in many cases and only share a short vacation. Many employees are transferred to remote postings or sent abroad for extended periods of time and, all too frequently, they do not bring their wife and children along. To this can be added a huge generation gap, which will be referred to later, that makes communication difficult between family members even when they do meet.[11]

Another social activity that was highly rated by the survey was socializing with friends. In just about any other society, this is hardly a problem. In Japan, it most definitely is. It is not only that employees put in long hours. They are expected to socialize primarily with their colleagues and not outsiders. Partly, that is desired by other colleagues, but it is also company policy so as to increase harmony or whatever. Thus, it is unseemly for company members to explain that, no, they do not want to go for a drink after work. They want to spend time with their boy or girlfriends, or chums from school, or people they share cultural, social or other interests with. Seeing such outsiders is almost like cheating and must be done furtively if one does not want to get into trouble.

Not surprisingly, there are relatively few neighborhood or voluntary activities. Again, by the time most employees get back home, it is too late to do anything and, anyway, they are too tired. Weekends are not much better, and that has to be spent with the family. So there is not much social or charitable action. Boy Scouts, Little League and the like do not flourish. It is even getting difficult to continue the local festivals, where they exist, or initiate them in the newer districts.[12]

But at least such occupations are not frowned upon. Workers who engage in political activism would be in more serious difficulty with their employers. This would not only occur if they joined Communist, Socialist or trade union groups but for conservative ones as well. The basic idea is that, by expending time and energy on some outside cause, no matter how worthy, there is less left over for the company. This equally applies to religious commitments if they absorb too much time or make excessive social demands.

It is not even as if, by minding one's own business and going one's own way, complications could be avoided. Loners and individualists are not highly appreciated in Japan, whether by the company or anyone else. Yes, a hobby is all right. So is some sport. But there is precious little time or energy left for thinking deeper thoughts or seeking inner paths. Those who do are quickly marginalized and often shunned or, as the Japanese put it, become a protruding nail that must be hammered in.

What is perhaps most depressing, because it was an integral part of Japanese tradition and doesn't really hurt anybody, is that people have been uprooted from nature more than anywhere else in the world. Concrete has invaded the cities, urbanization has spread, and there is pitifully little nature around. It is still missed by older folks, especially those who grew up in the countryside. This is already sad enough. Sadder is that many youngsters don't even know what nature is and, far from treasuring it, they avoid or scorn it.

What with one thing and another, the quality of life could hardly be regarded as good, as suggested by Bill Emmott. Certainly, it is not as good as in the West, or much of Asia, for that matter. And it is not regarded as good by the Japanese. It is therefore not surprising that most people should complain about unsatisfactory lifestyles and inadequate *yutori*. Will things be appreciably better in the future? One would have to be a hopeless optimist, a Japanese politician or a foreign sycophant to claim so.

Old Age Insecurity

If most Japanese are rather dissatisfied with their present quality of life, they become considerably more nervous and distressed when they think of what their old age may be like. That is what saps any relative contentment and *yutori* more than anything else. And this is not without cause. Japan's social security and welfare system have repeatedly lagged needs and are certainly not geared to the requirements of the late 20th century, let alone the 21st.

Opinion polls have consistently reflected a note of concern. One, by the Modern Comprehensive Research Think Tank of the Economic Planning Agency, was quite revealing. According to it, over 40 percent of the respondents felt that they would lead "an austere life." Nearly half thought they would lead an old age "comfortable enough to give pocket money to our grandchildren." But only 9 percent expected to have enough money to take trips in Japan or abroad. Where would that money come from? Very few assumed they could rely on their children. Most supposed that their living expenses would be covered by public pensions. Alas, since a couple needed ¥3 million a year to get by and this was substantially more than they could obtain from the state, they may have been optimistic even in their modest hopes for the future.[13]

As even the more doting admirers conceded, the Japanese social security and welfare system leaves much to be desired.[14] It was developed later than in Western countries and never expanded quite as much. In fact, during the 1980s, when the system should have been reinforced, it was actually cut back. Today, it provides less coverage and fewer benefits than in other advanced countries. Tomorrow, when it will really be needed, it will probably prove even more inadequate.

Of its various components, the health care side looks most impressive. It absorbs over 6 percent of gross national product, a figure that has risen swiftly and is about the same level as in the West. There are almost (but not quite) as many physicians and beds per 1,000 inhabitants as in other advanced countries. Particularly significant, everybody is covered by health insurance. They do not all belong to the same scheme, and some are more ample than others, but at least there should be little concern about the need for medical care . . . unless the government continues raising the share paid by the beneficiaries.

However, the figures can be misleading, especially for comparisons based on the amount of money spent. The Japanese system is uncontrolled, with patients visiting doctors as often as they want and doctors prescribing whatever medicine and treatment they want. Moreover, the cost of medicine is relatively high. This has led to massive abuses with the Japanese logging more visits than anyone else and doctors happy to pocket the fees. They further augment their earnings by overprescribing costly drugs, which benefits them directly since they often double as pharmacists. The winners are not the patients but the physicians and pharmaceutical companies.

So the amount of money disbursed is no measure of the system's performance.

Social security and welfare, on the other hand, clearly lag behind other advanced countries. The ratio of social security expenditures to national income has remained low, at 14 percent in 1988, compared to 16 percent in the United States and from 25 to 40 percent in European countries.[15] Not surprisingly, the benefits are smaller with Japanese under the employees' pension scheme drawing 41 percent of their average wage in 1989 while Americans got 45 percent and most Europeans from 40 percent to nearly 60 percent in Sweden.[16]

It must be fairly obvious that 41 percent of average wages would be inadequate to enjoy a comfortable old age. That has to be rounded out from other sources. One supplement would be the pension provided by the company, sometimes a lump sum, increasingly an annuity. Yet, despite all the lip service paid to workers, the amounts are only substantial for long-time employees of larger companies. There is little or nothing for those whose career was brief or truncated or who worked in temporary or part-time positions as well as employees of small companies and the self-employed.

Next, of course, comes personal savings. Most foreigners assume that the thrifty Japanese are prodigious savers and thus have accumulated a comfortable sum by retirement. Often enough, this is true, and many elderly couples have as much as ¥20 million, although the average level is lower and some are quite bereft. In addition, although not as well known, people have been accumulating more debt than ever, so what is left over may be more modest. Still, no matter how large, it must be remembered that with today's life expectancy, the money may have to cover twenty years or more. Thus, on the whole, savings are just a marginal aid.

Land and a house can be far more valuable . . . if they can be traded in for something. After all, you still have to live somewhere. Thus, some old folks sell their house and move into an old age home. Others strike a deal with the children: you get my house if you look after me. No matter how attractive in material terms, ever fewer children are staying with their parents and there are already nearly 4 million households consisting of senior citizens or couples living on their own. That the situation is not as cheery as might be hoped can be seen from a rash of suicides by senior citizens, many committed because they did not want to be a "nuisance" to the family.

The only other way of rounding out the budget is to continue working. Japan has the largest number of workers over the age of 65 and every opinion poll shows that senior citizens want to work. While the *tatemae* may be to keep occupied or benefit society, the *honne* is usually that they need the money. Once again, however, not all elderly persons can work because they lack the skills or cannot find a job. Or the available jobs are too exhausting or demeaning or simply do not pay a living wage. Finally, an increasing number are just too old or senile.

It should be mentioned that, although money is clearly crucial, a suitable old age support system requires more than that. There must be sufficient, properly equipped facilities. There must be old age homes, special clinics and all sorts of sophisticated paraphernalia to treat asorted afflictions. There must also be enough personnel. Both the facilities and the personnel presently are and will probably remain sorely inadequate. That is because land costs for such facilities are too high and it is hard to get staff since many of the jobs are relatively unpleasant, require long hours and do not pay well.

What about the future? Will the situation improve? That is hardly likely for three reasons: demographic, financial and political.

Over a decade ago, the Japanese became alarmed by the rapid aging of the population. With people living ever longer, and Japan actually holding the record for longevity, the share

Portion of Population 65 Years Old and Over by Country, 1900–2025

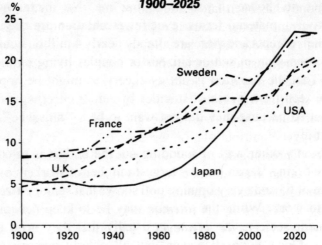

The only thing that's growing fast in Japan nowadays
is the aging population.

Source: Institute of Population Problems,
Ministry of Health and Welfare
Credit: *Facts and Figures of Japan 1991*, p. 14.

of elderly was steadily growing. By 1990, they accounted
for 12 percent; by 2020, that should reach 23 percent. But
at least then the birth rate was high enough to maintain a
stable population. Now, however, the birth rate has slumped
to one of the lowest, with later marriages, later childbirths
and fewer children. This means the demographic structure
will shift even more dramatically than expected.

Obviously, with an increasing share of older pepole and a
decreasing number of young people, the working population
will shrink. There will be fewer and fewer Japanese working
to support those who are retired. By 2000 there might be only
four, and by 2020 just three, compared to over six at present.

That would ruin the economics of any system. But one where little money has been laid aside and much of the cost is paid out of current contributions is especially vulnerable. That is the kind of system Japan has. So, by the year 2020, when Japan has the most aged society in the world, there will simply not be enough money to go around.

This shortfall can only be filled in two ways, neither of them particularly appealing. Either the existing workers must make bigger contributions or the aged must derive smaller benefits. Unfortunately, given the speed of the demographic shift and Japan's lag, minor changes will not be enough. Over the coming decades, payments will have to double to somewhat over Western levels or retirement benefits will decline further to very sub-Western levels. The bill will run into not billions but trillions and tens of trillions of yen.

This raises the political question. Which solution will the Japanese opt for? Companies have long resisted higher taxes and social security levies because this would hurt them financially. They are already frantic about the present high level and many feel they could not survive if taxation rose to Western heights, let alone further. Ordinary citizens are divided. Workers do not want to pay more taxes. The elderly want more funds. But they are not organized. There are no associations of aged or retirees which could lobby effectively for improved benefits or even hold the line at the present level.

As for the politicians, although many of them are already decrepit enough to be retired, they take the easy way out by just doing nothing. Perhaps nothing is not the right word. When there is enough pressure domestically or from abroad, they improve the system somewhat. When that pressure relaxes, or taxes cannot be raised, they cut back. Meanwhile, due to ever more persons getting ill or retiring and drawing on the health and social security schemes, costs rise implacably. Rather than act, the government issues papers

Social Security Expenditures

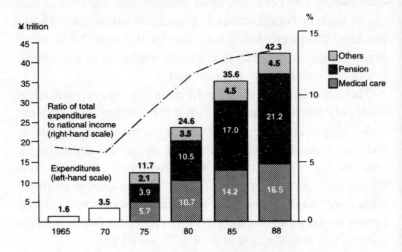

Just imagine how much it will cost in another
decade, or two, or three....

Source: Ministry of Labor, *White Paper on Health
and Welfare*, 1991.
Credit: *Facts and Figures of Japan 1991*, p. 74.

about the challenge of aging, reaffirming its aim of creating
an open-minded and affluent society, full of vitality and
social harmony. But it does not vote a budget to achieve
this.

No wonder the aged are worried. They know that the
chances of improvement are slight and the odds that things
will get worse considerably higher. They do not know
exactly what will happen but one of them suggested that,
as in the war, they would be placed on half-rations. Or
they might be sent to remote areas or even old age colonies
abroad, as MITI suggested. Whatever the solution in each

individual case, old age is unlikely to be a time of fulfillment
for most.

NOTES

1. Bill Emmott, *The Sun Also Sets*, p. 57.
2. Economic Planning Agency, *White Paper On Livelihood*.
3. *Yomiuri*, January 4, 1991.
4. Ibid.
5. *The Economist*, January 5, 1991, p. 28.
6. *Yomiuri*, February 12, 1991.
7. *Yomiuri*, July 8, 1990.
8. Prime Minister's Office, *Public Opinion Survey on the Life of the Nation*.
9. NHK Public Opinion Research Division, *Survey on the People's Distribution of Time in Daily Life*, 1991.
10. Prime Minister's Office, op. cit.
11. For more on the family, and other social institutions, see Jon Woronoff, *Japan: The Coming Social Crisis*.
12. For more on social problems, see Tadashi Fukutake, *Japanese Society Today* and *The Japanese Social Structure*, and Rokuro Hidaka, *The Price of Affluence*.
13. *Yomiuri*, February 6, 1989.
14. See Kent Calder, *Crisis and Compensation*, pp. 349–75.
15. Ministry of Health and Welfare, *White Paper on Health and Welfare*, 1991.
16. Ibid.

8
The Human Element Fails

Eroding Work Ethic

As everybody knows, much of Japan's economic success can
be traced to the human element. Its people were hardworking
and sacrificed for the good of the country. They were disciplined and put their personal needs and interests second.
They showed exceptional loyalty to the company even at cost
to their own personal or family life. All these characteristics,
which were very real, contributed mightily to the economy's
rise.

But this commitment should not be exaggerated. Nor
should it be assumed that such characteristics and virtues are
immutable or eternal. Like any other people, the Japanese
can change and not all that change will be for the better. So
much is readily admitted for Americans, and Europeans, and
other Asians. For the Japanese, however, many admirers
claim that the work ethic will not soften. Such a kindly—
and misguided—view was expressed by Frank Gibney,
among others, in an essay on "the work ethic and how it
grew."

"Where do Japanese workers differ? Won't they lose their
old-fashioned work ethic, as we seem to have lost ours, as
they grow more 'individualistic' and 'leisure-oriented'? As

their standard of living rises, won't they want to see working hours go down and vacation times lengthen so they can extend their searches for individual fulfillment, leaving the company premises after five as desolate as their American counterparts? I believe they will not."[1]

That is, to put a nice face on it, pure *tatemae*. The reality is quite different. In Japan, generation after generation has moved away from the supposedly inherent and innate Japanese work ethic. This has been a gradual process. It has also been a continuing one, with each generation taking a further step. To bring things up to date, I must mention a few additions since this book's predecessor.[2]

Back in the 1950s and 1960s, most employees had been hardened by the war and inured by the postwar difficulties. They did not expect much and were quite willing to accept necessary sacrifices. They worked diligently and put in long hours as a matter of course. They became the celebrated "workaholics" and company men we have heard so much about, known locally as *moretsu shain*. But these company "warriors" were already being replaced by younger Japanese, for whom the wartime deprivation was a faint memory and who increasingly had been brought up in a fairly soft and comfortable society.

Sacrifice meant little to them. What they wanted, and that can be easily understood, was a better home and family life. Work was all right, but it was not everything. So the "my-home" and "new family" cohorts tried to increase their independence. Alas, they needed money to lead the comfortable life they sought, and that kept them busy. New groups, which were even more individualistic, gradually replaced them. Since they did not care that much about work they were often referred to as the *shirake sedai* (reactionless generation). But the latest batches actually dislike the situation enough to distinguish themselves from the rest by calling themselves the *shin jinrui* or "new human race."

While admitting the existence of generational change, some observers claim that it has no lasting effect. This is just a passing phase among youngsters who will eventually grow up and become *shakaijin* (responsible adults and members of society). The work ethic will therefore be maintained at an acceptably high level. While comforting, that thought has little reflection in the realities of the workplace. There has been a notable relaxation in the intensity of work and many emerging practices are clearly undermining the economy.

One rather blatant manifestation of the eroding work will took the form of the sort of jobs youngsters would accept. In bygone times, they regularly went into manufacturing. Of late, that has become decidedly less popular, with more opting for financial and other services. Even students with engineering diplomas have sought jobs with banks and brokers. Further down, it is getting ever harder to find ordinary factory workers and more older women have had to be hired, with or without the skills. Meanwhile it has become pretty certain that the situation will only worsen. Graduates increasingly shun what they call the "three-K" jobs, those which are *kitanai, kiken* and *kitsui* or dirty, dangerous and demanding.

Aside from this, workers of both sexes and all ages have been avoiding small companies. There are obvious reasons for this: wages are lower, hours are longer, vacations are shorter, job security is lesser and, to top it all off, many of them have all three Ks. The situation for many is getting desperate as their workforce ages and cannot be replenished. In recent years, employers were unable to recruit the newcomers they needed and some will go out of business for lack of labor. By the way, many of Japan's farmers, shopkeepers and artisans will also disappear without successors.

Another sign is that younger salarymen are less interested in promotions and certainly do not strive to attain them as their predecessors did. One explanation, a perfectly rational one, is that with companies expanding more slowly there are fewer managerial posts to go around and the chances of reaching the top are smaller. But even if they could get a promotion, many youngsters would not actively seek (and might conceivably avoid) it if this entailed too much more work, responsibility or social pressure. Repeated opinion polls have confirmed these trends.

Naturally, it is not easy to evaluate the intensity of work. Are people plugging away or just coasting along, doing no more than necessary? Such distinctions are harder to make for Japanese, since they have been schooled in making believe they are disciplined, industrious and loyal. Yet, there is more than enough anecdotal evidence that younger workers do not put everything into their jobs. Nor are they willing to give of themselves excessively, avoiding company functions and activities. If this means they will be paid somewhat less or get fewer promotions, so be it.

What was once covert behavior has gradually become more overt. Like it or not, companies have had to concede that not all employees were willing to do or die. They therefore created a two-track system with two career paths: *sogo shoku* and *ippan shoku*. The former is a career-track position leading upward into management. The latter is a general track, leading nowhere in particular. Those who accept it can put in fewer hours, skip company socializing, and enjoy more independence in exchange for slower promotion, smaller wage hikes and perhaps earlier retirement. While not intended for men, and markedly less rewarding, many men have opted for the general track and, in so doing, opted out of the traditional Japanese system.

What do young workers want? That is not a mystery, not in a country that is constantly generating polls to measure swings in opinion. On the positive side, many want challenge and an opportunity to display their abilities. Some seek this even if it does not lead to increased wages or promotions.

They also want jobs that are clean and comfortable, involved in fashionable areas, and offering more leisure. That was summed up in three other Ks: *kankyo* (pleasant environment), *kaiteki* (comfortable conditions) and *kyuka* (plenty of paid vacations).

Much is made of these moral aspects, by foreigners and by Japanese. That is partly a *tatemae*. The honest *honne* is that material considerations play a significant, probably decisive role. Job-seekers, especially college graduates, check very carefully on what wages and perks they can get. This is becoming easier since dozens of magazines survey the major, and sometimes smaller companies, and indicate down to the nearest yen what the starting wages are, how they have been evolving, what the future prospects are. They provide insight into allowances, bonuses and frills. Through friends or contacts, it is possible to ascertain what the dormitories, sports facilities and health care are like. There is little sentiment involved here and the choice is hardheaded and almost ruthless. So, in all honesty, it is indispensable to add a fourth K, namely *kane* or money.

This will doubtlessly explain why the Japanese are not as optimistic as foreigners about the preservation of the work ethic. Rokuro Ishikawa, president of the Japan Chamber of Commerce and Industry recently complained: ''Young people today are more interested in making money than in creating and building things. They only want the easy jobs—where they don't have to work or get their hands sweaty.''[3] Factory supervisors and office managers gripe that it is getting harder and harder to teach newcomers the ropes and, no sooner do they learn, than they move on to another job. The older generation as a whole gossips about the laziness, laxity and egoism of today's youngsters. Meanwhile, youngsters staunchly insist that they will not be sucked up by the company the way their parents were.

Applying to become labor aristocrats.

Credit: Foreign Press Center/Kyodo

Decaying Loyalty

Many foreigners, admittedly often the more naive, seem to think that loyalty is an inalienable virtue of the Japanese. They gladly serve their employer, or the state, or whatever, and are satisfied with the moral rewards this brings. Such loyalty, it is argued, reaches far back into Japanese history and was shown by the *samurai* to their lords, the lords to the *shogun,* and the people to the emperor. The epitome of this virtue, we are told time and again, is the story of the forty-seven *ronin* who selflessly laid down their lives for their defunct lord.

Nowadays, this loyalty has been transferred to the company. Workers supposedly serve the company because of the inner satisfaction that brings as well as the knowledge that they will be looked after by the company in return for this display of loyalty. Indeed, according to some management gurus and other romantics, there is almost a bonding between company and workforce. This has been expressed by Ezra Vogel, William Ouchi and other supposed authorities.[4] The version of Gene Gregory, long a reporter for the *Far Eastern Economic Review*, is quoted here.

"Workers and managers alike identify themselves with the goals of the enterprise, and their most important identification is, reciprocally, the name of the company for which they work. They belong to the enterprise in the same sense they belong to a family and, as in the family, a living reciprocity of obligations and rewards binds them to the enterprise in common destiny. As they are strongly identified with as well as by the goals of the enterprise, members are moved all the more strongly to try to improve it. Identification as the primary reward becomes the operative motivation."[5]

There is no doubt that loyalty is exceedingly important in the Japanese management system. It is routinely urged and praised by corporate executives, sometimes using language that would be familiar to ancient lords and retainers. But it is much more than lip service, the whole seniority system (*nenko-joretsu*) is structured both to encourage and reward it. For example, the wage scale is tied to length of service, with employees earning increments each year. They also receive semi-annual bonuses, a more rudimentary way of rewarding those who stay on. Since promotions come with the years as well, as one rides the career escalator, loyalty brings loftier titles, greater prestige and enhanced authority. Companies do this despite the fact that, as we already noticed, the system decreases efficiency and expertise.

Japanese-style management, which rewards loyalty more than any other national system, was created by both management and labor because both stood to gain. Employees were relieved of fears of dismissal or penalties affecting wages and promotions. Employers knew they could count on personnel sticking with them through thick and thin and could therefore deploy them more effectively, alter jobs and tasks more readily and expand whenever desired. It became possible to invest in costly training since those who underwent it would be around long enough for the company to benefit. In short, it permitted a long-term approach to running a business.

But the support of both parties has varied. Initially, shortly after the war, it was the trade unions that pressed for job security since losing a job then would be horrible given massive unemployment and widespread poverty. Employers only gave in grudgingly, since they could easily replace lazy or incompetent workers. During the 1950s and 1960s, or whenever there was a boom in specific sectors, it was in the interest of the company to hold on to workers. For the latter, switching to another job was often tempting. In recessions or when industries declined, on the other hand, employers did not fancy lifetime employment quite so much.

Thus, during the 1970s and 1980s (and doubtlessly into the 1990s as well), there was little compunction about getting rid of workers one way or the other. What distinguishes Japanese companies from foreign counterparts is who gets the sack first. The initial reaction is to reduce recruitment, but not entirely since younger employees are more energetic and cheaper. Then part of the peripheral staff is dropped, namely temporary and contract workers, part-timers and homeworkers, and workers supplied by outside firms. Women are also disposed of more rapidly than usual. Meanwhile, to keep their own employees busy, big companies take in work that was previously done by suppliers and subcontractors, leaving them to dismiss labor.

If this is not sufficient, albeit with some regret and much rhetoric, even personnel who supposedly benefit from lifetime employment are dismissed. When possible, this is done gently, by offering "voluntary" retirement with generous compensation. If that is not accepted, and there is still excess staff, the next round of offers is less generous and employees are warned that, if they do not go then, they may actually be fired. Other employees are transferred to subsidiaries, suppliers and subcontractors, again leaving them with the problem. In a pinch, companies even set up special subsidiaries into which they dump the redundant staffers, with lesser responsibilities and wages. In the last instance, however, they do fire deadwood, which usually consists of the old (and costly), incompetent, ill and women.

Workers can also be disloyal on occasion. Even more deplorable, there has been a tendency among employees to downgrade the very idea of loyalty in seeking, holding or leaving a job. Loyalty may be a traditional Japanese virtue, youngsters may have heard the story of the forty-seven *ronin* until they are sick of it, and juniors may be bribed, coaxed and coerced by their seniors, but there are other elements involved as well. Thus, as Kunio Odaka explains, drawing on extensive personal observations:

"Only the uninformed outsider, or nationalist seeking something to extol in the Japanese character, could believe that all Japanese have some kind of innate loyalty that would prevent the disintegration of the company even if nothing were done to strengthen and consolidate personal relations. . . . Today as in the past, Japanese who work for a company work for their own needs and interests. If they work willingly, it is because the work satisfies their own needs and does not involve any undue suffering or sacrifice."[6]

What are these other elements? What are the needs and interests of Japanese workers? One of them, actually quite important although it is usually downplayed, is purely material. As was noted, wages increase from year to year. Consequently, anyone with enough annual increments would be tempted to stay, all the more so since he would probably have to start much further down elsewhere. The calculation is quite sober and was presented in a report of the Asahi Mutual Life Insurance Company. If a worker changes jobs at age 25, it will cost him ¥29 million in his lifetime income. If he changes at 35, the loss will rise to some ¥58 million. And so on.[7]

Another consideration derives from the deployment of generalists and use of in-house training. The result is that most employees, including managers, do not have any expertise or skills they could sell on the labor market. All they know is what the company taught them, and it is only useful within that company and nowhere else. Other companies have meanwhile trained their own staff in what they regard as useful and would therefore see little point in hiring outsiders. Anyway, there is a tacit agreement among major companies not to poach from one another and thus defectors would be poorly received and probably have to settle for a lesser job in a lesser company.

Those who are most tempted by material rewards are therefore fresh recruits who have not yet gained much seniority and would not take much of a loss if they changed jobs. They would also find it easier to seek employment due to their age and the fact that a new employer could still shape them. But the driving desire is often moral rather than material. More and more young workers are dissatisfied with the present system. Those who are more dynamic or competent do not want to advance on the escalator all together, a step at a time. They want to be rewarded for their personal ability and contribution to the company. That is a more radical demand and, as one of Japan's leading management experts, Keitaro Hasegawa indicated, could have devastating effects.

"The younger generation wants to be paid and promoted according to ability, and it does not want to wait for recognition until the spring of each year. The members of the new breed feel that it is only fair to reward a successful project or improvement in performance with an immediate pay hike. They are too impatient to wait for their turn to come in the conventional schedule of promotions by seniority. Unless top management realizes that young workers are united in the belief that on-the-spot rewards are the very soul of meritocracy, Japanese-style management . . . will be undermined by massive defections."[8]

Further up, among the middle-aged, the dissatisfaction is becoming more acute. During the period of rapid expansion there were plenty of new openings and just about everyone who stayed on the escalator could become a manager, even if it were necessary to create new jobs with titles but no functions. With slower economic growth, and bloated hierarchies, companies have been forced to reduce the number of managerial positions and many will be passed over. Yet, that is why they joined and worked for the company. In addition, wages are not rising as much at the upper end, so the material rewards are less impressive. Thus, older employees also think seriously of quitting although, as they have fewer opportunities, this remains just daydreams for most.

Whatever the causes, the effects are perfectly unmistakable. Employee loyalty is on the wane. This can most readily be measured by the increase in job changing (*tenshoku*), which has corporate management worried. Almost 9 percent of the workforce changed jobs in 1990. That is perhaps not much compared to the West, but it was the highest level in

Japan's recent history. More significant is that job-hopping has been growing steadily among younger workers and could spread as they age. Meanwhile, more workers than ever were toying with the idea of switching jobs and probably would since alternative opportunities were also multiplying.[9] Particularly ominous was a poll by Japan Recruit showing that 49 percent of workers aged 20–24 wanted to change jobs in 1990 compared to 38 percent in 1985.[10]

Even more appalling than job-hopping is that many graduates were no longer seeking regular employment. They much preferred continuing the temporary occupations they had become accustomed to as students. They became known as *furita* or "freeters," a combination of the English word "free" and the German word for "worker." It is hard to know how many freeters there are but the number is growing and the practice is becoming more acceptable. One survey showed that well over half of the college students liked the concept.[11]

Gaping Generation Gaps

Naturally, these changes in attitudes toward work and the company have to be seen on the much broader background of social and attitudinal changes in general. Despite all the loose talk about Japan preserving its roots and carefully absorbing the best of the new into the old, there have been very striking dislocations over the years. In fact, without exaggeration, there has probably been more variation from generation to generation there than anywhere else. And the generation gaps are so large there is little hope they can be bridged.

That would be only natural. Older people were brought up in an incredibly regimented society, one which worshipped the emperor and sacrificed for the nation. They were then drawn into a war which made the utmost demands on loyalty and abnegation. The defeat, to a Western opponent, was a terrible blow to Japan's sense of superiority and, for some at least, generated a brief inferiority complex. That was quickly thrown off as the economy gathered speed and affluence appeared. More recent generations, already well over half the total population, know almost nothing of the war, the postwar deprivation and the self-doubt. They have been brought up in comfort and regard continued ease as a goal, if not a right.

In such a rapidly changing social, political and material environment, how could there not be sweeping changes in people's attitudes? That such changes have occurred was shown by every survey undertaken. The only reason that more stress is not placed on these changes is that, during the past decade or so, they have not given rise to alarming manifestations like the anti-war and anti-growth movements or the open criticism and radicalism of earlier periods. Today's youths appear fairly tame, relatively satisfied with the status quo, less eager to push and shove to get what they want. But what they want is even more different from what earlier cohorts sought.

Some of the most significant trends can be seen from Japan's oldest nationwide opinion survey, the Study of the Japanese National Character conducted by the Institute of Statistical Mathematics. It has been undertaken every five years since 1953 and even has prewar forerunners. The relevant question allows respondents to pick the most congenial lifestyle from among five alternatives which were summed up as interests, comfort, wealth, propriety, civic spirit and honor. Among these five, there have been definite winners and losers.[12]

One of the losers is the rather traditional one of honor, namely that one should study seriously and establish a reputation, a choice hardly ever taken nowadays. Another has been civic spirit, to lead a life devoted entirely to society without thought of self, chosen by 10 percent or less since the war although the number two choice before. A further, even more popular prewar goal was propriety, to lead a pure and upright life, resisting the injustices of the world, which has slipped gradually to about a tenth of the respondents. Oddly enough, wealth, or the urge to work hard and make money, never did terribly well, although it has fared better than the previous spiritual goals. The real winners were comfort and interests. The second most popular goal was to lead an easy life in a happy-go-lucky fashion and the outright winner was to do what you find interesting, regardless of money or honor.[13]

For anyone who dotes on continuity in Japanese mores, it should be noted that this was a complete reversal from prewar to present times. It spawned the various social trends and categories referred to above, such as the my-home and new family contingents. It has come down to the current situation where today's youngsters pointedly distinguish between themselves, the *shin jinrui* or "new human race" and their elders, the *kyu jinrui* or "old human race." Admittedly, commentators differ as to the salient characteristics of each, but the gist is pretty clear. The older generation includes the corporate warriors, those who would sacrifice family for company, self for nation. They were relatively thrifty and lived quite modestly. These are not youth's goals. They manifestly want to lead their own lives in their own ways and do not want to be subject to company or state. They also want comfort and will pay for it.

One knowledgeable observer, Hikaru Hayashi, senior research director of Hakuhodo Institute of Life and Living has summed up the *shin jinrui* lifestyle under six main traits. First, they tend to base decisions on personal desires rather than logic. Second, they value comfortable, non-confrontational relationships with others and these relationships are amiable but shallow. Third, while going their own way, they do enjoy forming groups. Fourth, almost everything they enjoy, such as traveling abroad, requires considerable funds. Fifth, to get these funds, they are willing to work, but they want their leisure. Finally, the *shin jinrui* do not want to grow up and prefer putting off the responsibilities and restrictions of adulthood.[14]

While not easy to generalize, the Dentsu Institute of Human Studies divided them into two categories, "epicurean egoists," who value their own benefits most, and "cooperative individualists," who place equal priority on their relationship with society. The latter are thus more traditionalist, the former more of a deviation. That is important because, according to the DIHS report, within twenty years the "epicurean egoists" should be the more numerous. And that would create serious social problems for Japan.[15]

Although it is impossible to know exactly how these changes will impact society, certain trends are already evident. With regard to work, several have been mentioned. There is bound to be more job mobility and less company loyalty. Graduates will pick jobs they like and, if they change their mind or don't get along, move on. As one said, "I don't really care if I have to keep changing jobs as long as I eventually find a company that will allow me to develop my abilities."[16] In so doing, they will shun the three Ks of dirty, dangerous and demanding while seeking the three other Ks of environment, comfort and vacations, plus the fourth, money.

There will be other changes with regard to consumption. Those have already become quite noticeable and were seized upon by Japan's retailers, always eager to make a fast yen off youngsters who spend with much greater abandon than their parents. This is extremely important because, from even the most superficial reading of the times, it is evident that the younger generation is extremely materialistic, when not epicurean. That could be seen from the money thrown at luxuries of all sorts, especially those that were fashionable.

Young women were the best (worst?) performers here, spending more on name brand clothing, accessories and travel than their counterparts abroad or Japanese young men, who do however show expensive tastes in cars, watches and booze. A more studied analysis come from Mariko Sugahara, director of the Consumer Statistics Division of the Management and Coordination Agency.

"Public opinion polls confirm that young consumers in particular have clear preferences with regard to apparel and accessories. Unlike their elders, they look to clothing to make a statement about their individuality. This tendency is not limited to females; today's young males are also fashion-conscious. From now on, apparel is expected to rank along-side cars among the items young people most want to spend on. Whereas older Japanese see furs, imported cars and other such luxuries as too extravagant for their tastes, young Japanese do not agree. Their purchasing power should keep the trend toward greater diversity and higher quality in motion."[17]

If Japanese youngsters are spending more than before, the next question must obviously be where they get the money from. Part of it is earned. Starting wages are higher than before and, to someone who has just left high school or college, must seem like a fortune. That is especially so if they still live with their parents, as many do, and do not have to pay for housing and many meals. They can, if they want, devote almost all of their earnings to spending. Most women go in for shopping in a very big way. More of the men hold back, partly for social reasons, partly to put money aside for a house and family.

Increasingly they are spending more than they earn. Regrettably, in addition to substantial savings, many Japanese now have substantial debts. The debts are actually rising faster than the savings. This can be traced to widespread use of credit cards. Younger shoppers tend to have more and use them more frequently than older ones. And some apparently go too far. The number of delinquencies is growing rapidly and the number of Japanese who have declared personal bankruptcy for this reason has risen sharply. Indeed, believe it or not, a recent report by the Economic Planning Agency showed that Japan's consumers had piled on more debt per person than Americans.[18]

Beyond the personal tragedies this can cause, it is contributing to a long-term decline in the savings rate. It has fallen from 23 percent of personal income to only 14 percent over the past two decades. By the year 2010, according to the government, it should drop to 9 percent and perhaps less. Part of that can be attributed to dissaving by retirees who will need the money to get by. Another, less welcome share, can be traced to youngsters for whom thrift and savings are not very highly evaluated. Less savings, of course, means that it will be harder and more expensive for companies to come by the money they need to operate and grow.

Important as they are, the effects on work ethic, consumption and savings may not even be the most important. One underlying trend, a very powerful one, has been the move toward individualism, a very radical change for the Japanese. This has been frequently decried by spokesmen of the *kyu jinrui,* from dad and mom, to grandpa and grandma, to the president of the Japan Chamber of Commerce and Industry. He angrily criticized the growing sense of "me-ism" in Japanese society. "There has been a weakening of personal discipline and civic responsibility," he complained. "We see only self-exaltation these days—not just in industry, but in government and education. There is a pervading tendency to value money and materialism too highly."[19]

Whatever they may think of such comments, there is no doubt that the old social fabric is being torn apart. People are no longer willing to belong, to contribute, to sacrifice. They do not trust the existing institutions, the company, political parties, bueaucracies, even the family. But they have not been able to reform or replace them. The younger generations actually seek friendly and cooperative relations, they want more informal and less hierarchical ties, they could perhaps even create a better society one day. On the other hand, since the establishment does not allow them to fashion their own new world, they refuse to adhere to the old. Thus, Japan's society could collapse or implode and drag the economy down with it.

NOTES

1. Frank Gibney, *Miracle by Design*, p. 78.
2. For more on generational change, see Jon Woronoff, *Japan: The Coming Social Crisis.*
3. *Business Tokyo*, October 1991, p. 64.
4. See Ezra Vogel, *Japan As Number One*, William Ouchi, *Theory Z*, and others.
5. Gene Gregory, "The Logic of Japanese Enterprise," Japan Productivity Center, *Strategies for Productivity*, Tokyo, UNIPUB, 1984, p. 117.
6. Kunio Odaka, *Japanese Management*, p. 26.
7. *Japan Economic Journal*, August 30, 1986.
8. Keitaro Hasegawa, "The Upheaval in Personnel Management," *Japan Echo*, Vol. XVII, 1990, p. 24.
9. See "Job Mobility and Work Attitudes of Young Workers," *Japan Labor Bulletin*, February 1991, pp. 4–8.
10. *Financial Times*, September 24, 1991.
11. See Yamana Kazuma, "Recruit and the Age of the Temporary Worker," *Japan Echo*, Vol. XVII, 1990, pp. 42–7.
12. Institute of Statistical Mathematics, *Study of the Japanese National Character*. See also Sumiko Iwao, "Recent Changes in Japanese Attitudes," Alan D. Romberg (ed.), *Same Bed Different Dreams*, New York, Council on Foreign Relations Press, 1990.
13. For more on these social trends, see Rokuro Hidaka, *The Price of Affluence.*
14. "A Kinder, Gentler Generation," *Look Japan*, April 1991, pp. 4–5.
15. *Yomiuri*, December 23, 1990.
16. "The Crumbling Walls of Lifetime Employment, *Tokyo Business Today*, September 1988, pp. 28–9.

17. Mariko Sugahara, "Consumers in Pursuit of the Good Life," *Japan Echo*, Vol. XVII, 1990, pp. 57–60.
18. *The Economist*, March 9, 1991.
19. *Business Tokyo*, October 1991, p. 64.

9
Work Is No Fun

The Company "Family"

Not only is Japan supposedly blessed with a wonderful work ethic, it apparently has workers who—contrary to most others—positively like working. Vogel not only claimed that the Japanese have made large organizations "something people enjoy," but that "employees come in to their workplace on vacation and weekends in large part because they enjoy the camaraderie."[1] The Morgans blissfully cite a model employee who "feels a sense of fulfillment from his work and his company and cannot imagine ever leaving. . . ."[2] And Thomas J. Nevins, a labor trouble-shooter for foreign companies, dotes on just how much the Japanese enjoy working.[3]

On the basis of many years experience working alongside Japanese, whether in my own company or others, I have not noticed any unnatural love of work. But I have noticed that the attitude toward work varies strikingly with where one is located in the labor force. After all, the context is quite different in large and small companies, for permanent and temporary employees, for factory and office workers, for men and women, for younger and older staff. That is normal. But the differences tend to be greater in Japan because the labor force is more hierarchical and structured.

Obviously, life is best at the top. The top, in Japan, means a major or first tier (*ichiryu*) company. There are many reasons for this. The premises are usually more comfortable and spacious, the pace somewhat more sedate and, above all, there is the prestige that goes with it. Of course, status is not everything. Employees of these companies normally put in fewer hours and enjoy more leisure, the work is not as hard and demanding, there is more machinery to accomplish unpleasant or tedious tasks. Most important, job security is incomparably greater. The chances of such companies going under are minimal and those of dismissals only slightly larger.

All of these factors vary for smaller companies, working your way down from fairly large, to medium-sized, to small and even tiny. With each step, the premises are less attractive, the pace more hectic and the status diminished. Employees work more hours a day, more days a week and more weeks a year. They get stuck with the unpleasant tasks that large companies do not have to or do not want to handle. To make things worse, job security is very relative, acceptable during booms, doubtful during busts. For then, smaller companies have to contract or go under.[4]

That is the situation in general. In comparatively independent companies, there is a possibility of improvement over the years. Dependent companies, on the other hand, are affected not only by the vagaries of the economy but the whims and wishes of their overlords. Such dependent companies include suppliers, subcontractors and distributors of major companies, especially those tied into a vertical or distribution *keiretsu*. Although the former are sometimes referred to as the parent firms (*oya-gaisha*) and the latter, children firms (*ko-gaisha*), this relationship is not always a caring one and, in a crunch, the smaller firms are more likely to suffer.

Thus, to keep its own workers from doing 3-K jobs, the parent company may dump them on suppliers and subcontractors. To give its employees more time off, it may force its assorted children companies to work around the clock and on weekends. Indeed, under the just-in-time (*kanban*) system, they are tied to its rhythm and have little leeway. Worse, they serve as a buffer in hard times, cutting back while the prime contractor takes in work and even, on occasion, they have to absorb its excess staff. As for distributors, they work long hours anyway but do not even determine their own margins, which obviously affect what kind of premises, wages, hours and security they can provide. A fine extended family this is!

Even within each company, large or small, independent or dependent, the situation differs greatly for each category of labor. The privileged members of this family are the regular employees (*sei-shain*), those who presumably have steady work and "lifetime" employment. I say presumably because a permanent job is not written into the contract, it is tacit, just assumed, and can be evaded in various ways. Still, whether truly permanent or not, regular employees clearly get the choice posts, the best premises, the backup and equipment, the most normal hours and, last but not least, the highest status.[5]

Aside from regular employees, there are many other types. There are temporary workers, those who are hired to do a specific job for a specific time, usually a job that regular workers do not particularly like, and can be laid off on shorter notice or whenever their contracts run out. There are part-time workers, who put in a specific number of hours and, like other temporaries, usually get stuck with the less pleasant jobs under less congenial conditions. Their contracts can also be terminated, hours reduced . . . or increased. For part-time is often a misnomer since many of them work long hours and also put in overtime. They are just hired as part-timers to avoid greater commitments.[6]

Going a step further, there are what is known as "outside" workers (*shagaiko*), another misnomer, since they work inside the factory or office alongside regular staff. The crucial difference is that they are provided by other firms, usually to do the most disagreeable tasks, those that cannot be assigned to regular, temporary or part-time employees. They frequently have very irregular schedules and may be sent from job to job with considerable frequency. The most tenuous group, however, consists of piece workers who are paid a small fee for work, usually quite nasty work, accomplished. This is often done in their own homes, with the help of family members. Jobs only last as long as work is provided and can thus be terminated at a moment's notice.

Within these various categories, it is necessary to distinguish between white-collar (*shokuin*) and blue-collar (*koin*) workers. While conditions in modern factories have improved, they are still harsh compared to those in modern offices, especially in the luxury headquarters buildings in the city. True, the salarymen and managers do put in long hours, but the intensity of work is considerably less. The chances of their losing their job and having to find a new one, within or outside of the company, are much smaller since the pace of automation and rationalization is much slower. Moreover, being closer to the boss, they manage to delay cutbacks and dismissals more effectively, although some may eventually get sacked.

Then come the many distinctions between male and female workers. While men often work more intensely than women, that is because they are given genuine responsibilities which enhance their prestige. Anyway, almost by definition, the status of men is higher than women. While, both in factories and offices, women do not get the most grueling tasks, they are customarily relegated to the most tedious. The most glaring difference concerns job security. Almost a third of the female employees are "irregulars," namely temporary, part-time or fixed-term staff. Even those who get regular posts are not ordinarily regarded as permanent personnel. It is assumed that they will resign at marriage or childbirth and, if they do not, pressure is brought to bear more often than not. Just like the traditional Japanese family, and society, there is substantial inequality. Male, white-collar employees in large companies fare better than all other categories. Second in line, although with a bit of a gap, are male, blue-collar workers in large companies. They are the ones who benefit most from the system, so much so that they are sometimes referred to as the "labor aristocracy." The rest are just commoners and subjects, if not serfs and pawns.

This should lead one to question the widespread idea that the happy company family with workers enjoying lifetime employment is somehow typical. It is far from that. The only ones with anything approaching guaranteed job security are the labor aristocrats and even then it is not ironclad. The rest are probably not much better off than workers in the West, where hire-and-fire is more the norm. Sometimes, they are even worse off, if they are very peripheral workers or employed in very small or dependent firms.

How many benefit substantially from lifetime employment and all the frills? That is hard to tell. At best, they are a minority, and probably a rather small one at that. After all, large companies only account for 1 percent of the total with 20 percent of the labor force, although other companies with perhaps another 20 percent emulate them. Even they have numerous temporary, part-time and outside workers plus a large contingent of females. The labor aristocrats could hardly exceed 15 to 20 percent of all workers. That is not, by my reckoning, enough to make this "typical" system very typical.

A far better way of describing Japan's management is as a "core" system. Regular workers in larger companies form the core. Within these companies, they are supported by any number of more dispensable workers, who form a vast peripheral labor force. Meanwhile, the larger companies form the core of corporate groups consisting of their subsidiaries, suppliers, subcontractors and distributors. They inevitably do the bidding of the core and form another type of periphery. The closer one is to the core, the better one fares. The further away, the less fortunate one is, with the peripheral workers of the peripheral companies worst off.

This idea of a core has another advantage. As intimated, it is a more durable emanation of Japanese culture. There has always been a core that dominated Japan, whether under lords, *shogun* or emperor. This structure was taken over by warring corporations. It should continue even if lifetime employment and other characteristics were to cease. For, unlike the frills, it can adapt to changing economic conditions. The core can expand in good times and contract in bad. But it is most unlikely to disappear entirely.

Blue-Collar Blues

There is no question that blue-collar workers are highly efficient and productive. They work very hard and are flexible and adaptable. That has been demonstrated by every study made by foreigners or Japanese.[7] It can also be verified by visits to Japanese factories, which always prove an eye-opener to foreigners who marvel at just how "busy" the workers are and how much more they accomplish than the miserable lot back home.

Whether those concerned are happy about this is another matter. Some maintain that they are. They often belong to the "culturist" school which claims that many aspects of Japanese culture have incited hard work and pleasure in working hard. Others adopt a "corporatist" approach, in particular Ronald Dore who assumes Westerners will eventually emulate the Japanese in providing "welfare corporatism" including "factory and company based trade union and bargaining structures, enterprise welfare and security, greater stability of employment and integration of manual workers as 'full members' of the enterprise, greater bureaucratization and a cooperative or corporate ideology.''[8]

Unfortunately, foreign observers and pundits all too rarely bother asking Japanese workers what they think. When they do, alas, they get answers which are totally at odds with what they expect. For it turns out that Japanese workers are not very happy. They are not as happy as one would presume with lifetime employment, assorted welfare frills and modern machinery. They are not even as happy as foreigners, who do not have as much job security, welfare frills or modern machinery. This has been shown by some of the more honest comparative studies, especially by those who actually worked in Japanese factories.[9]

However, in my perverse view, the best evidence comes from a recent comprehensive study of work organization and work attitudes in Japan and the United States by James R. Lincoln and Arne L. Kalleberg.[10] They set out to demonstrate that Japanese workers are more committed to their companies and more satisfied with their jobs than Americans, a standard and widespread assumption. The results they obtained, alas, showed the opposite.

With regard to work commitment, the Japanese almost systematically proved less committed. For example, in response to the statement "I have other activities that are more important than my work," 44 percent of the Japanese agreed as opposed to 31 percent of the Americans. Turning to organizational commitment, the situation was even worse. Only 54 percent of the Japanese but 74 percent of the Americans were "willing to work harder than I have to in order to help this company succeed." Only 58 percent of the Japanese but 64 percent of the Americans were "proud to work for this company." And merely 19 percent of the Japanese but 42 percent of the Americans felt "my values and the values of this company are quite similar."

This was nothing compared to the scores for job satisfaction. When asked, "all in all, how satisfied would you say you are with your job?," only 18 percent of the Japanese were positive versus 34 percent of the Americans. When asked, "how much does your job measure up to the kind of job you wanted when you first took it?," barely 5 percent of the Japanese were positive versus 34 percent of the Americans. And, when asked, "knowing what you know now, if you had to decide all over again whether to take the job you now have, what would you decide?," just 23 percent of the Japanese would come back while as many as 69 percent of the Americans would do it again.[11]

Why should Japanese factory workers be so uncommitted and dissatisfied? The first place to look at is productivity and how it is obtained. There may be a price to pay. This price may be paid mainly by blue-collar workers. And the price may be too high.

For one, to be certain that production is maintained at sufficiently high levels and flows at a steady and foreseeable rate, quotas have been established. Often the workers are expected to participate in determining them, but they do not have much input. The amount of work is more a function of demand for the product, the availability of labor and facilities and, above all, what is being squeezed out of workers in competing companies. Given the competitive element, the tendency is to have very high quotas which are gradually ratcheted upward. Workers who do not achieve these quotas face "withheld praise, enforced overtime or reprimands."[12]

In achieving the quotas, ever more is expected of the workers, especially under the "Toyota system" which has spread throughout Japanese industry. For starters, workers are constantly busy because there are no time reserves. It is necessary to get the job done within the time alloted and, in order to ensure that, the whole line is kept moving at a pace that is punishing for newcomers or weaker members. There are no longer buffer stocks so that, if something goes wrong, there is no leeway to correct it. There is no relief manpower or standby labor so that if someone is absent, sick, on holiday, or just has to go to the toilet, there is no one to cover for him. Worse, in many cases, there is not even enough manpower to do the job comfortably so everyone has to make an "extra effort."[13]

The most sinister aspect of the system, however, is that whatever the killing work pace today, tomorrow it will be worse. To the managers and supervisors, that may appear to be a laudable, continuous improvement of productivity. To the workers, alas, it looks more like an endless and pointless rat race they can never win. That was clearly expressed in this comment by a jaded worker, quoted by Satoshi Kamata in *Japan in the Passing Lane*.

"Now the work is nearly three times tougher than when I came here six or seven years ago. . . . And they keep speeding up the line. The faster the line gets, the harder we work to catch up, because we want to go home quickly. But when we finally get used to the speed, then they make it even faster. Right now it's a minute and fourteen seconds per unit, but I bet they'll speed it up. The new guys can't handle it any more. You read in the newspapers that Toyota workers are quick and active. We're not quick. We're forced to work quickly."[14]

This is only part of the story. Quality is the other side. Japan is justifiably proud of its impeccable quality standards. But they impose an additional burden on the workers since the responsibility for quality is placed on them and not special quality control staff, as in the West. Say what you will, it is not easy to make a dozen or more quality checks while attaching parts or adjusting products, minute after minute, day after day, week after week. It is even harder when the line speeds up and quality standards are also raised.

Yet, workers are expected not only to assure quality as

A suggestion a day keeps the supervisor away!

Credit: Toyota

part of their job, they are expected to help the company enhance it through quality control circles and suggestions. This participation is seen by many outsiders as signs of work commitment and job humanization. Sometimes, especially in earlier years, they probably were. More recently, participation has been anything but voluntary as quotas are set for the amount of QC work done or number of suggestions submitted and, while those who make special efforts receive faint praise or petty rewards, those who do not are chastised and could lose their job.

In other countries, workers faced with such treatment might resist or turn to the unions. In Japan, they do not. There is no point to it. The unions, by and large, have become mere adjuncts of management and rarely espouse serious griefs.

They would most certainly not bring pressure to bear by going out on a real strike. So, most rank-and-file workers do not even consult them. Again, in the words of an ordinary worker:

"And the union, they're supported by our money, but they only work for the company. You can't expect anything from them because the leaders are all general foremen. They change every year, so nobody has enough time to get into the job seriously. If you complain to them, they just tell you to 'cooperate' and say, 'Unless you produce more your salary will not go up.' "[15]

You would think that the evidence were sufficiently convincing to make a case that Japanese factory workers really are not happy and that they have valid causes for this. But foreign admirers, echoing Japanese managers, have pat answers. For one, there is the cultural element. Japanese workers, or so it is claimed, have greater expectations so when things do not work out as well, they are dissatisfied. Also, they do not know how truly horrible things are in the West. If they did, they would be pleased with their lot. Still, until proven otherwise, there is no justification for assuming that Japanese workers are incapable of expressing their feelings and, if they are dissatisfied, there must be reasons.

If that line does not work, the apologists insist that, yes, indeed, there were abuses in the Japanese system. But that is a thing of the past. The situation has improved enormously since. That is what Dore claimed in his unconscionable introduction to Kamata's book. But Kamata, on returning to the Toyota factory, found the situation worse rather than better with the work pace and compulsion more forbidding than before. Now there is talk that "lean" methods have made factory work more efficient and also more humane. True, there is less brute force. But there is more monotony than ever.

What has not changed, nor is likely to change, is that blue-collar workers are pushed harder than white-collar employees and managers. They will continue making the biggest contribution to Japan's prosperity while benefiting relatively less. Rather than being treated as "full members," they will still be treated as subordinates who have to be directed by their betters. Finally, in response to this situation, workers will remain dissatisfied with their lot and youngsters will flee the factory.

White-Collar Blahs

Naturally, one would expect morale to be much higher in white-collar or salaryman circles. After all, they are a relative elite and enjoy definite advantages. Yet, the results are quite similar. In a recent survey by the Prime Minister's Office, only 41 percent of research workers found their work interesting.[16] Other polls got much the same response. And that could be borne out by conversations with any Japanese employees you may know (especially over a drink).

Not only are Japanese salaried employees not particularly happy, as for the factory workers, they are unhappier than foreign counterparts. In one survey, by the Ministry of Labor, only 58 percent of the young Japanese said they enjoyed their jobs compared to 85 percent of young American and British workers.[17] Even more damning was a broad Harris poll covering fifteen countries. In it, only 17 percent of Japanese office workers were satisfied with their jobs, the lowest rate of any country. By contrast, 43 percent of the Americans were very satisfied. The Japanese were also uncommonly disgruntled over pay and benefits, management and supervision, and job challenges.[18]

While a lot of this is relatively diffuse, generalized discontent, some of it is directed against the company as such. That should be obvious to anyone who has eavesdropped on Japanese salarymen having a drink with colleagues or friends after work. In fact, they seem to have no end of gripes against superiors, subordinates, co-workers (some of whom are competitors for promotion) and, of course, the boss. While the company rarely asks their view, a recent poll is very revealing. More than 70 percent of the personnel at Yamaha, the leading musical instrument maker, responded that they would not suggest their relatives work there nor, if they had it to do over, would they work for the company again.[19] That Yamaha was not alone in this predicament was confirmed by a broader survey which showed that a majority of retiring salaried employees would choose a different company the second time around.[20]

Given this kind of feedback from the Japanese themselves, the task of any honest researcher should not be to explain away the complaints or to relativize them but to seek the causes for this widespread and deep-rooted dissatisfaction. Some of the explanations follow. But there is much more for those who seek the truth.

Perhaps the first step should be to realize that Japanese-style management does not appeal to everyone. Some like it, some do not. Even among the Japanese, there are persons who are more cooperative and others who are more individualistic, some who do not mind having Big Brother look over their shoulders, others who abhor it. For them, the controlled and restricted life of even the most prestigious company is stifling. This was nicely explained by Kunio Odaka, whose book on Japanese management is uncommonly frank and revealing.

"This system appeals, however, only if the employee is able to find work that suits him within the corporation and the corporation is willing to let him pursue it (and very few employees are so lucky), or if the employee is content to be an ordinary salaried worker satisfied with whatever work, rank, and treatment the corporation assigns him. For such employees, lifelong employment was and is extremely beneficial, and no doubt they would agree heartily with the saying that 'a big tree gives the best shelter.' But to a person who cannot satisfy his personal needs in the company, who suffers from the feeling that he has gotten into the wrong place by mistake, and who would like to find a company that offers more congenial work and change careers before it is too late, lifelong employment can seem more like life imprisonment— a cruel system whose motto is 'Abandon all hope ye who enter here.' While lifelong employment contributes to employment stability, it is a source of considerable unhappiness for some people."[21]

What about harmony (*wa*) which we are told enjoys the very highest priority in Japanese society? When it is relatively spontaneous, harmony can be delightful. But it rarely is. More often than not it means wearing down those who disagree, buying off those who can be coopted and simply ignoring or expelling those who refuse to go along with any decisions. It can result, in Japanese parlence, in hammering in the nail that sticks out. This means that the never-ending quest for *wa* can actually contribute to the discomfort and frustration of many workers, even those on the winning side.

Aside from this, there are all sorts of specific complaints which anybody, from any culture, can easily understand. Hours worked are, indeed, very long. The intensity may not always be great, but the cumulative burden is more than many can endure. Work relations, despite every effort to make them harmonious, are not always smooth. However, with lifetime employment, rather than get away from bothersome colleagues by moving to another company, you have to tolerate them throughout a career. In return, the pay is not really generous and there are genuine worries about life after retirement. All of this has been dealt with elsewhere, so there is no need for further elaboration.

What is more interesting to consider here is that, at different periods in the salaryman's life, there are different problems and discomforts. We have already noted that many young recruits do not like riding the escalator, not if they are more capable, dynamic or ambitious. They may even leave if they get too frustrated. Still, once through the first decade or so, they tend to accept that they will stay with the company for the rest of their career and, in so doing, gradually move upward.

That was once a safe assumption. It no longer is. So, for the maturing employee, the biggest source of anxiety is whether he will actually get a managerial post or, at least, a title. To satisfy as many people as possible, during the 1960s and 1970s, companies actually created jobs and titles, some with absolutely no responsibilities and petty wage increments. But a bloated middle-management was no longer feasible during the tougher 1980s, and they had to cut back. The present prospects of riding the escalator into oblivion are more than many can take.

And oblivion really is the word. Many aging staffers get "promoted upstairs" to consulting positions. Others get "promoted sideways" to subsidiary occupations like salesmen.[22] The most grotesque case is the so-called "window-side tribe" (*madogiwa zoku*). These are employees who are given a title and a desk by the window, but no responsibilities and no subordinates. They just sit there all day and gaze out the window or, if they have any gumption, quit. In most cases, let it be mentioned, those who do not make it also take a substantial loss in earnings, ranging from one-third to half of their former salary.

There is another relatively discreet way of getting rid of deadwood. That is to send less useful employees, many of them already getting on in age, to a remote local or foreign office. Frequently, whether because of the children's schooling or because the company did not provide enough funds to take along the family, these transferees live alone and have created a numerous category of *tanshinfunin*. During their years away, most live quite miserably in company dorms or meager quarters, visiting their families on rare occasions. Many suffer from depression or alcoholism. Yet, to refuse the post would reduce any chances of promotion and perhaps result in dismissal.

Yet, even those who do attain managerial positions are not always happy. The responsibilities are enormous. Middle managers, your *kacho* and *bucho,* are not only expected to oversee and direct subordinate staff. They have to do their own job as well. And they have to socialize. They must go drinking with clients and suppliers, with superiors if they want that next promotion, with underlings if they don't want disaffection in the ranks. That requires immense time and effort and creates psychological strains. No wonder so many managers suffered from nervousness, sleeplessness, ulcers and a rather amorphous *kacho-byo* or *kacho's* disease.

More recently, this has taken a turn for the worse. As the core shrinks, the *kacho* and *bucho* are saddled with ever greater responsibilities. If they are serious, ambitious or dedicated, the company takes advantage and makes them do more and more work, sometimes more than they can handle. That has resulted in something far more serious, *karoshi* or death from overwork. Under the strict definition of the Ministry of Labor, there are only about a hundred cases a year. *Karoshi*-monitoring groups counter that there are thousands, as many as 10,000 a year.[23] This includes instances where employees had to put in excessive overtime, forgo weekends and holidays, or travel incessantly for the company.

Meanwhile, there is increasing fear of *karoshi* among ordinary workers. They complain of assorted but unremitting ailments, sometimes imaginary, sometimes all too real. This was conveyed by a survey of Fukoku Life Insurance. Some 43 percent of those polled stated that they were worried about being stricken with *karoshi.* Among those employees, 44 percent said they felt 'stressed,' 44 percent complained of

Business and pleasure, pleasure and business.
It just never ends.

Credit: Foreign Press Center/Kyodo

constant fatique, 28 percent lacked creativity and motivation and 23 percent wanted to call in sick.[24]

At least, or so one would assume, they benefit from lifetime employment and job security, unlike Western workers. Alas, as many elderly workers have learned to their regret, there has been some erosion. By the age of fifty, it really is a question of up or out. Out can take the form of actual dismissal. But it is more often a matter of being shifted to a lesser position within the company or, more likely, a subordinate position within one of the subsidiaries, suppliers, subcontractors or distributors. The company may also set up special firms in entirely unrelated sectors, perhaps a fast food outlet or leisure center, which it subsidizes for a while as a "retirement home" and then leaves on its own.

While some "spiritual" bond may be maintained, it is clear that these are now second-class employees. They receive lower salaries, put in longer hours and often have to relocate. Worst of all, they are given orders by younger staff. Thus, more timorous salarymen live in dread of that "tap-on-the-shoulder" (*kata-tataki*) by management. Hardier ones try to learn a skill, develop a specialization, anything that could enhance their attractiveness. Then they look for another employer. But few come up with anything interesting. After all, as was noted, most do not have much to offer and, despite any respect for the aged, employers prefer hiring younger staff.

Such is the fate of all too many white-collar personnel. That does not mean that there are not very contented ones, too. They can be found among those who are not ambitious and are quite willing to do whatever the company wants as well as those who grew with the company, rose to the top and achieved their ambitions. In between, however, there are countless salarymen who are not very happy with their lot and have good reason not to be happy.

Working Women's Woes

In only one area, of the many discussed in this book, has there actually been an official reform. That occurred with regard to female workers whose situation was not only poor but generally perceived as such. For years, Japanese feminists and to some extent the trade unions had urged improvement of this status. But it was not until the United Nations Decade for Women, from 1975–85, that international pressure was added. Finally, after much hesitation, the Diet adopted an Equal Employment Opportunity Law which came into force in 1986.

The day of its enactment, April 1st, may have been symbolic. For, as with so many "reforms," it was another case of two steps forward, one step back. Only this time, it may have been two or three steps back. First, in order to get the legislation passed, women had to sacrifice earlier gains, like limited night work and restrictions on dangerous jobs. They also had to accept gaping loopholes, like permission for employers to advertise for male or female personnel for specific jobs. Only those open to both sexes would be covered. Secondly, the legislation did not include any legal penalties for violation. Employers were simply asked to do their utmost to ensure equal treatment. If they did not do so of their own free will, there was no way of making them obey the "law."

Third, and worst, employers promptly set about finding other means to the same end. What they eventually hit upon was a two-track system whereby employees could choose between career-track (*sogo-shoku*) or general-track (*ippan shoku*) positions. The former led upward into management, the latter led nowhere in particular. Employees, admittedly, could decide which track to take. But there was enormous pressure on women to select the second. Management warned that the first implied long hours, unpleasant tasks, weighty responsibilities and, if all else failed, sudden transfers that could disrupt the family. They were told, in one instance, "if you are transferred tomorrow to a remote area, can you leave your husband and children here? Your family will fall apart."[25]

In this sense, the "reform" clearly made the situation worse than before. Previously, women simply underwent discrimination which was imposed from above. Now they had to make a fateful decision and, if they opted out, it was henceforth their fault. That was compared by one feminist to the "stepping tablet" which Christians had to tread when renouncing their faith.[26] In practice, the vast majority of women did renounce their hopes and dreams of a career and enter the general track. The supposed gains of the equal opportunity law were thereby sacrificed.

Nonetheless, women continued joining the labor force in

Women's Work-Force Participation by Age, 1989

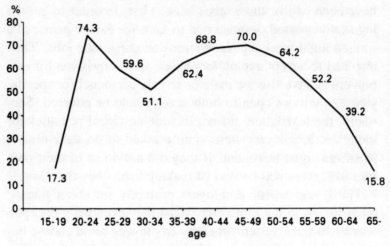

Why working women are either young and cheap
or old and cheap.

Source: Ministry of Labor, *Facts on the Female
Labor Force*, 1990.
Credit: *Facts and Figures of Japan 1991*, p. 56.

large numbers. By 1990, about half of all women were working and women accounted for some 40 percent of total employment. The new dispensation did not put off young women either. According to surveys of high school and college seniors, the vast majority wanted to get a job. And most of them apparently intended to stay with the company indefinitely. That they did not was obvious from the fact that the M-shaped employment curve remained. There were large contingents of young female workers, then a notable dip as many retired to bring up a family, followed by another hump—an ever growing one—as women returned for a second stint at work.

What happened to them during those periods was not always pleasant. Again, treatment differed considerably between blue-collar and white-collar workers and also between the first and second jobs.

Young women have always been sought after by the factories for their vigor and dexterity. They can do the minute and repetitive tasks required by assembly lines, especially in machinery and electronics. Since most of them are only high school graduates, and many are country girls, they are relatively docile. They can be easily directed, moved from place to place and, if need be, laid off. They are not likely to militate for improvement and often participate eagerly in quality control circles, seen almost as a social activity. Their reward is to put in long hours, doing tiring and painstaking labor, for rather modest wages . . . until they are no longer wanted.[27]

The situation for young women in the offices is different in certain respects. They have a good education, in many cases just as good (or better) than the men they are working with. They come with somewhat greater aspirations of developing their abilities and pursuing a career. But most are quickly relegated to second-rate tasks. While usually not very strenuous or demanding, certainly not compared to factory work, they are often demeaning. And the office ladies (or OLs) do not appreciate their status. With little likelihood of changing the situation, and blocked from a career if they have opted for the general track, they often react with indifference to work and devote more energy to spending the money they earned in agreeable ways. This has earned them the reputation of an "OL nobility" (*OL-kizoku*).[28]

Older women who have returned after raising children fare much worse. There is no hope of a career and most are starting at the bottom again even if they had spent years working before. For the factories, their fingers are not sufficiently nimble and they get clumsier, grittier tasks. In the office, there is hardly a trace of them, since OLs are expected to be young and fresh, the "flowers of the office." Many therefore end up in distribution, whether working at the counter or trudging around town making door-to-door sales. The worst off, as indicated, are the many piece workers who do hopelessly tedious tasks at home.

If a tear should be shed for the younger workers, and two for the older ones, certainly the greatest pity is deserved by those who buck the system. Some women have firmly decided that they will stick with the company, they will pursue a career, and they will make the exceptional efforts required of women to achieve what many men accomplish just by riding the career escalator. These career women, first of all, have to show superior drive and performance. They must also prove that they can handle any job a man can, despite sexual stereotypes. To succeed, as one female manager explained, you have to ''think like a woman, act like a man, and work like a dog.''

That is only one facet of the effort. The other is more social and personal. In practice, many of these career women cannot raise a family or even get married, since Japanese men expect their wives to be homebodies. At work, they are undercut by male colleagues who do not like being shown up by women and fear that they may not get that next promotion as automatically as thought. Men also do not like taking orders from women or serving under them, since it might entail a loss of status. Worse, there is little support from other women. Most OLs find career women a bit coarse and grubby, certainly not the feminine creatures they now have as role models. So, they either spurn or spite them.

Despite strenuous efforts by dedicated women, the results have been quite disappointing. Many women are only promoted to posts where they deal mainly with other women, whether as clients or subordinates. They are rarely given serious responsibilities. Even in lower managerial ranks, there are not many of them, and most of those are working in cosmetics, fashion and retailing, women's sectors in short. Further up, there are few to be found. Less than 1 percent of the *kacho* and *bucho* are women and there are only four presidents in the 1,264 listed companies.[29]

Once again, these are not just the views of a critical foreigner. The material here was gleaned from works by Japanese specialists, most of them women. The facts are relatively clear and generally accepted by women and men, trade unions and the government. Moreover, there are now excellent studies in English of the general situation or actual working life of Japanese women, most of them being relatively sober and somber.[30]

Nor does one have to impute any dissatisfaction, that can be gathered quite readily from conversations with women or between women. If you want more formal data, let it be mentioned that, in a recent survey by Philip Morris K.K., 55 percent of the women said they were not being treated equally with men at work.[31] In a five country study carried out in Japan by *Nikkei Woman,* Japan made a lamentable showing against the United States, Germany, Australia and even Brazil. Japanese women were by far the most dissatisfied with their jobs (one out of three complaining as opposed to one out of six elsewhere). Only a third of them found their work interesting and fulfilling, less than elsewhere. And one out of three even admitted to crying over work at least once a month, usually because of poor interpersonal relations.[32]

Here, too, Japan has achieved less than other advanced countries. Elsewhere, women do have more opportunity, often written into laws that are enforceable with penalties that make employers follow the rules. There is still discrimination, but it is not institutionalized into a two-track system. More women are pursuing a career, more are rising, and more have become managers and executives. To do so, they can remain women rather than becoming surrogate men, and they can lead an otherwise normal life.

Will things be better in the future? The politicians swear that improvement is on the way. Bureaucrats merely affirm it. And businessmen are unwilling to commit. As for women, they really do not expect much. In the Philip Morris poll, just a third of the female workers thought their lives would improve over the next two decades.[33]

NOTES

1. Ezra Vogel, *Japan As Number One*, p. 235.
2. James C. and Jeffrey J. Morgan, *Cracking The Japanese Market*, p. 68.
3. Thomas J. Nevins, *Labor Pains And The Gaijin Boss*, Tokyo, Japan Times, 1983.
4. See Norma J. Chalmers, *Industrial Relations in Japan, The Peripheral Workforce*, and Kazuo Koike, "Workers in Small Firms," in Taishiro Shirai (ed.), *Contemporary Industrial Relations in Japan*, pp. 89–116.
5. This was confirmed by Kazutoshi Kochiro, Professor of Economics at Yokohama National University. "Generally speaking, the workforce in most industries consists of an upper one-third of regular workers who enjoy job security, good wages, and safe working conditions. The remaining two-thirds of the workforce are relatively poorly paid, have less job security, and are more subject to work-related accidents." Shirai, op. cit., p. 83.
6. Mary Saso, *Women in the Japanese Workplace*, pp. 144–5.
7. See, among others, Robert E. Cole, *Japanese Blue Collar: The Changing Tradition*, Ronald P. Dore, *British Factory, Japanese Factory*, and Dorinne K. Kondo, *Crafting Selves*.
8. Dore, op. cit., p. 370.
9. See Cole, op. cit., Kondo, op. cit., and Satoshi Kamata, *Japan In The Passing Lane*.
10. James R. Lincoln and Arne L. Kalleberg, *Culture, Control and Commitment*.
11. Lincoln and Kalleberg, op. cit., pp. 64–5.
12. Richard J. Schonberger, *Japanese Manufacturing Techniques*, New York, 1982, p. 29.
13. See Knut Dohse, Ulrich Jurgens, and Thomas Malsh, "From 'Fordism' to 'Toyotaism'," *East Asia*, Vol. 5, Boulder, Westview Press, 1989, pp. 24–9.
14. Kamata, op. cit., p. 144.
15. Ibid., p. 145.
16. *Yomiuri*, July 2, 1990.
17. *Tradepia International*, No. 41, 1990.

18. *Wall Street Journal*, November 19, 1991.
19. *Nikkei Weekly*, October 26, 1991.
20. *Yomiuri*, March 28, 1991.
21. Kunio Odaka, *Japanese Management*, pp. 63–4.
22. Chalmers, op. cit., p. 99.
23. *Financial Times*, November 29, 1991.
24. "Japan's Overworked Workers," *Wall Street Journal*, November 29, 1991.
25. "Women and Work," *Look Japan*, September 1990, p. 6.
26. *Yomiuri*, "Male vs. Female," January 8, 1991.
27. See Alice Cook and Hiroko Hayashi, *Working Women in Japan*, and Mary Saso, op. cit.
28. For more on the OLs, see Jeannie Lo, *Office Ladies, Factory Women*.
29. *Tokyo Business Today*, December 1991, p. 58.
30. See Cook and Hayashi, op. cit., Kondo, op. cit., Lo, op. cit., and Saso, op. cit.
31. *Wall Street Journal*, June 12, 1991.
32. *Nikkei Weekly*, February 23, 1991, p. 13.
33. *Wall Street Journal*, June 12, 1991.

10

Demise Of The
Classless Society

New Rich, New Poor

Japan is truly a land of myths. Nice, comforting, heart-warming myths, many of them tied up with a dynamic economy that offered people opportunity and brought equality. For example, not so long ago, a worldwide bestseller explained that "even today if you come to Japan you can see that there is virtually no poverty as it is known elsewhere in the world. You will find a kind of egalitarian society rare in the world, which the Japanese people prize."[1] Even the fact that this was written by Akio Morita, chairman of one of Japan's biggest electronics firm, Sony, and a dollar millionaire many times over, did not keep the naive from oohing and aahing.

Only now is the truth sinking in that, while there was a definite increase in opportunity and equality right after the war, trends over the past few decades have been in the opposite direction. There are now "haves" and "have-nots" and the latter contingent has been swelling quite noticeably of late. Once again, this is not just the opinion of an acerbic foreign critic, it was expressed by the official White Paper on National Life for 1988, issued by the Economic Planning Agency. In it, a poll revealed that not only were the Japanese aware of the negative trends, fully 74 percent of them felt that the system was unfair.[2]

The myth of equality has many props, but the most prominent is one segment of the annual Public Opinion Survey on the Life of the Nation which asks respondents to indicate in which class they would categorize themselves with regard to *standard of living*. As we all know, because it has been so widely publicized, an overwhelming majority of about 90 percent claimed to be middle class. Only 7 percent opted for lower class and less than 1 percent for upper class. What is less well known is that rather than three choices, they were given five: upper class, upper middle class, middle middle class, lower middle class and lower class. No wonder so many chose middle class! Even by pure random choice, that should have garnered 60 percent and, in a society that prides itself on nobody standing out, even more.[3]

This certainly makes that particular survey question one of the worst and most misleading ever conceived. Yet, even then, it is interesting to note that the share of the lower class has been growing, an ominous trend. More useful is another segment, this time asking respondents to categorize themselves with respect to *assets*. With that stipulation, about 15 percent opted for lower class and over 1 percent for upper class. They were no longer so uniformly middle class.

Further supposed evidence of equality comes from use of the Gini coefficient to show the relative level of five quintiles, with the gap from top to bottom rather small by international standards. The problem here is that it measures income rather than assets. It only "proves" that income is rather evenly distributed . . . not wealth. Assets are what determine wealth and heavily influence the reality of belonging to a specific class. When we look at assets, as in the previous survey, the results are much less encouraging. In fact, from 1980–87, the average value of assets owned by the top 20 percent more than tripled while those held by the middle 20 percent only rose modestly and, inevitably, those of the lower quintiles shrank.[4]

How could this happen? And why are assets such a significant indicator as opposed to income? Well, that can be easily understood by anyone who realizes how money is made in Japan. Those who work for a company and draw a salary have, as was noted earlier, obtained only a modest improvement over the years. With luck, wages kept up with economic growth or inflation. Those who charged fees that could be ratcheted up more rapidly or benefited from government largesse did considerably better. Those who invested in land, stocks and other assets made a fortune.

This latter point must be elucidated because it was not just a question of picking the right investments or being lucky. There was more to it than that. This was revealed to all by a series of scandals, the best known being insider trading at Recruit and compensation payments by Nomura and other brokerages. But the bubble economy was accompanied by countless other scandals and abuses.

As even the most superficial observer realizes, land prices have not ceased rising since war's end. Just counting from 1955 to 1990, the increase in values was astronomical. Prices for residential land in major cities had multiplied 210 times over while those for urban areas in general rose 83-fold. That can be compared to nominal wages, which only rose by a factor of 25, and not even half that when adjusted for inflation. Thus, anyone who invested in land, especially suitably located land, would have seen his net worth rise infinitely faster than someone who just worked for a living. Some who benefited were farmers, shopkeepers and others fortunate enough to have a plot of land. There does not seem to be anything intrinsically unfair about that.

The real money, however, was made by professionals. These were individuals and companies which bought and sold land like any other commodity. They could also locate plots

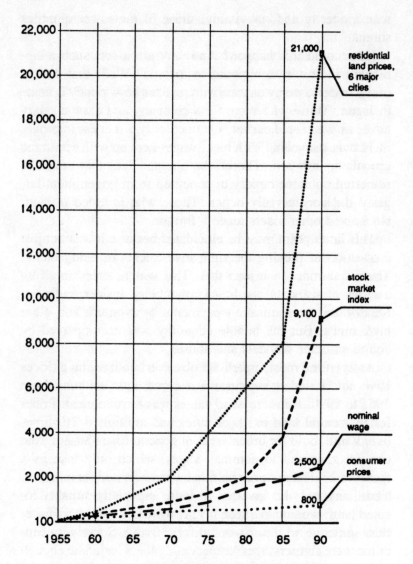

residential
land prices,
6 major
cities

21,000

stock
market
index

9,100

nominal
wage

consumer
prices

2,500

800

1955 60 65 70 75 80 85 90

"Investing" certainly beats working for a living!

Sources: Japanese Real Estate Institute, Economic Planning Agency.

Tokyo Stock Exchange, Ministry of Labor, Statistics Bureau.

which were most likely to appreciate. They might even consolidate the land, buying out the existing owners to piece together larger plots worth more. And they could acquire additional land by borrowing heavily from the banks. These professionals, many of them pure speculators, could increase their net worth by a factor of 100, or even 1000, if they were astute and well-connected.

That is somewhat different. Moreover, many of the land speculators had access to information not generally available, sometimes obtained from government sources through bribes. They displaced smallholders not only by offering good prices but using threats and violence. That they obtained huge credit lines from the banks seems reasonable, since they could offer land as collateral. But the amounts were so large, and sometimes so far out of line with the assets pledged, that they were excessive and occasionally obtained by fraudulent means. Meanwhile, the ordinary citizen was hard pressed to get a mere mortgage.

The situation for stocks was even more questionable. Admittedly, the Nikkei index only rose 91-fold from 1955 to 1990, and it underwent periodic corrections. But, smoothing out the fluctuations, it was still racing ahead incomparably faster than real wages. Moreover, unlike land, stocks were liquid and could be quickly bought and sold, enhancing the possible gains of "investors." Since relatively fewer persons owned stock than land, this meant that any gains were less broadly shared. As for land, the take could be extraordinary since stocks also reached "unreal" values, with price-earnings ratios in the sixties when they were closer to twenty in most other exchanges.

This already raised doubts about fairness. But the most dubious aspect regarded how shares were traded. In theory, anybody could buy stock in a listed company. If you thought the company had a good product, capable management or some other edge, you could invest and deserved to benefit.

Only, in Japan, shares were not traded on that basis. They were bought and sold more on the basis of inside information of one sort or another. Some of it came from those in the know within the companies. This led to many a windfall for them and their friends. More generally, the securities firms both issued and sold stock. They knew far better what companies were actually worth, and they traded on that information for themselves and favored clients. In addition, for initial public offerings, they could actually underprice shares and thereby guarantee that holders obtained fast and sure profits, as in the Recruit caper.

More disreputable is that stocks were frequently ramped or cornered by unscrupulous speculators. They would form syndicates that would pick a stock, buy it and run it up. Gradually, they would let in associates of lesser degrees, so that the run continued. When it had gone far enough, and ordinary investors or "suckers" bought the high-flyer, they pulled out with an assured profit. That is a nasty practice, but one tolerated in Japan. Worse, it was engaged in by the securities companies massively. They would inform their salesmen of which stocks should do well, first telling top staff, then others further down. They would first inform their best clients, then those further out. Naturally, once the buying began, prices shot up and attracted broader attention. Again, those who got in last, the "suckers," were usually small investors.[5]

The true scandal about the Nomura scandal is that it was limited to cases of "compensation," where the securities firms covered losses of important clients. That was disgraceful because they did not do the same for others, but it was not even illegal. Still, it did show clearly that the stock market was not actually a place where you could win some, lose some. Regulars won most of the time. They had inside information. They could ramp stocks. They could buy even more shares through loans from banks and securities firms.

In short, they could also increase their net worth by a factor of 100 or 1000 over the years. Those favored included many normal companies which engaged in *zaiteku* as well as many shell companies and speculators, some of them gangsters. Lastly, which may explain why this was done with such impunity, it included politicians who raised funds through "political stocks" and bureaucrats who were supposedly supervising the system.

Naturally, for the stock market to be rigged in favor of some, it had to be rigged against others. These were basically the small investors, many of them salarymen, housewives and retirees drummed up by an aggressive door-to-door sales force. Sometimes they won a bit, but hardly enough to justify the risk, quite often they lost. As we saw, they were the "suckers" who bought after prices had been ramped. They were also ripped off by their own brokers who engaged in "churning" or constant turnover of stocks to earn commissions. Worse, brokers often bought lousy stocks their favored clients wanted to dump and sold them to the small fry. Just how bad this could be was shown by the results of Japanese investment trusts (similar to mutual funds) which only appreciated by 4 percent a year during the 1980s boom when the index was rising 21 percent a year.[6] When the market collapsed in 1990, many were trapped and lost heavily.

No wonder so many ordinary Japanese felt the system was "unfair." They had another reason to complain of unfairness, too. Most sources of income were taxed, whether for the salaryman, factory worker, professional, shopkeeper or farmer. Not those of the land and stock speculators. Capital gains went largely untaxed. Moreover, when they were taxed, they were notoriously underreported. In the game of tax evasion, which is widespread in Japan, the tax administration regularly announced that vast sums were hidden by companies, including the most eminent. Equally miscreant were professionals, like doctors, dentists and lawyers. Even farmers found ways around the tax regulations. The result was the infamous 9:6:4 rule whereby wage earners whose taxes were withheld at the source paid taxes on 90 percent of their income, the self-employed only paid on 60 percent and farmers on 40 percent.

The outcome was a distinct polarization in terms of wealth. The Japanese themselves spoke disparagingly of the *nyuu ricchi* or "newly rich" who had amassed fortunes over the years. They were numerous. And they were often fabulously wealthy.[7] In fact, by the late 1980s, Japan had more dollar millionaires and billionaires per capita than America or Europe, although it had started with a fairly egalitarian society only four decades before.[8] The richest of the rich were usually land or stock speculators.[9] Owners of companies which developed the economy only came in a distant second. Further on down were the doctors, dentists and other professionals. There were also many politicians whose wealth was particularly surprising since it far exceeded what they could have earned legitimately.

In contrast, there were the *nyuu pua* or "newly poor." Most of them were ordinary folks, employees and factory hands, shopkeepers, tradesmen and farmers (unless they had excess land) and especially the staff of smaller companies or those in the peripheral sector. What often distinguished them from the rest is that they did not own a home, this category comprising some 40 percent of the population.

Mind you, poor means not only those with somewhat less than the average Japanese. There were also the outright poor, people who were dirt poor and frequently could not make ends meet. Some of them lived in slums in larger cities or the nastier parts of smaller towns. Others did not even have a roof over their heads and inhabited parks, underpasses, subway and railway stations. There were itinerants, and bums, and bag ladies. Indeed, it is hard not to see them unless you make an effort, which so many of Japan's well-wishers apparently do.

Those who did have a home, no matter how hard they had to work to pay for it, were still up there in the middle class. They consisted largely of the "labor artistocrats," those who worked for big companies and earned more, and could also have their mortgage guaranteed by the company. But it would be hard to claim that they actually led a middle-class existence as normally recognized abroad. As already explained, they lived in modest housing, far from their work place, put in long hours, had little vacation or leisure and not much security in old age. This made being middle-class in Japan very relative.

There were some others who were middle-class but led an upper-class lifestyle, as long as they could. These were the "bachelor aristocrats." That is, young men and especially women who still lived with their family and did not have housing expenses. They could therefore devote much of their earnings to shopping and leisure. Most visible were the young ladies, all dressed up like something out of a fashion magazine, and spending more in a week than their parents in a month. Once they got married, if they got married, that would have to cease unless both held a job, harder in Japan than elsewhere. So, they would probably be reclaimed by the "middle class" in due course.

One last aspect has to be mentioned here. It is geographical. Progressively over the years, Tokyo became the center for everything, government, business, finance, services, education, culture, etc. It therefore created a local economy that was more prosperous than anywhere else. This gap, too, was growing as Tokyo absorbed ever more of the wealth. In 1980, according to the Kansai Economic Federation, per capita income in Tokyo was 26 percent higher than in the rest of Japan. By 1986, it was 45 percent higher. And, by 1990, almost 60 percent higher.[10] This was another form of polarization that made claims of equality sound absurd, if not insulting.

Thus, by the 1980s, no matter what foreigners may pretend, the Japanese were fully aware of the existence of an economic and social gap or differential and *kakusa* became the latest buzzword. It was picked up by the government, it was disseminated by the media, and it was bewailed by the people, at least those who were on the wrong side of this gap.[11]

Whose Company Is This?

One area in which most foreigners seem to expect great equality is the corporate community. That is because so many gullibly believed the talk of life in the company as all of us together in the same boat. There are many things they overlooked, but the most noticeable is that there are obviously many boats and not all are the same. In fact, more than elsewhere, there is a distinct and strict hierarchy of companies.

The Japanese corporate community is dominated by large companies which, as was noted, do not even amount to 1 percent of the total. They have the largest capital, turnover, profits and personnel and the strongest political clout. They are often also the core of one or more groups or *keiretsu*, whether bank-related, manufacturing or distribution. Smaller associates are very dependent on them, especially suppliers, subcontractors and distributors. Beyond these groups, there are countless small to medium-sized manufacturers, wholesalers and retailers, service enterprises and others which are relatively independent but enjoy little government support. To regard them all as equal in any sense would be ludicrous.

It would be just as absurd to regard their employees as equal. Employees of smaller companies, among other things, put in longer hours, endure less pleasant conditions, earn lower wages and have less job security. Depending on size, wages vary from 20–35 percent less than in large companies.[12] The situation of workers who are not even regular employees of small companies, including many temporaries and part-timers could be much worse. At the bottom of the heap are assorted homeworkers paid miserly piece wages and who do not even have to be fired, they can simply be given no more work.

Even within the very same company, large or small, there are enough distinctions to make equality an exception rather than the rule. Like every other boat, you have the captain, and the bosun and those loading the hold. Companies purposely distinguish between "regular" workers, those who have access to steady employment and other advantages, and the rest. This "rest" can be employees who do the same jobs, in the same places, but are either on short-term contracts or under contract with an outside company. Many of them are part-timers, although they may be putting in as many hours as anyone else. Yet, they probably earn about two-thirds as much.

A further distinction arises between blue-collar and white-collar workers. The former are usually high-school leavers, the latter college graduates. The former earn considerably less, perhaps a quarter less than the latter, although as we saw they work much harder. Factory workers can be promoted to higher posts in the plant and maybe even further, but they will not climb as far as the salaryman class, whose members rise to the very top. Meanwhile, despite the official rhetoric, since they are less educated the blue-collar workers are treated as social and intellectual inferiors.

The final line is drawn between male and female staff. One way or another, women are usually given the least challenging jobs with the lowest status. They also earn far less. Part of this can be traced to seniority since wages rise with increased years in the company. But it is not the fault of women that they are obliged to resign young and earlier job experience is not counted when they return to the labor force. Nor, in many cases, is it their fault that they hold lower level jobs, many of them temporary or part-time. Still, whatever the causes, the results are perfectly clear. Women only earn about 60 percent as much as men. This is one of the biggest gaps among advanced countries as compared to 69 percent in the United States, 73 percent in Germany, 89 percent in France and 91 percent in Australia. Japan is also the only place where the gap has been growing while it shrank elsewhere.

Within the various groups, men, women, white-collar, blue-collar, large company, small company, there is another series of gradations. This time it is by seniority, not age, depending on when a person joined the company. These distinctions are very fine, and clearly demarcated, with those who entered one year earlier talking down to those just a year junior and up to those just a year senior. They are also paid different wages, due to annual increments, and hold different level positions, due to promotion through the career escalator.

Only here has there been some change, not so much with regard to promotion and status as wages. It has become so hard to obtain young workers that they had to be paid more and there were so many superfluous older ones that they were grateful to earn less as long as they were not dumped outright. Nonetheless, there is a distinct tilt to the wage scale, rising gradually during the early years and then peaking about the age of 50–55, before declining somewhat. The gap between the highest and lowest levels, while not as extensive as before, is still substantial (double or triple) and enough to hold on to most who have gained seniority.

Many of those who speak admiringly of equality refer specifically to the company situation. First of all, they insist, Japanese executives are not drawing fat salaries as in the West. Moreover, they add, Japanese executives do not earn much more than ordinary employees. This has been expressed by, among others, James Abegglen and George Stalk, Jr., in *Kaisha*.

"The *kaisha* provide more equal compensation throughout their organizations than is the case for companies in other countries. Extremes of compensation are avoided, and thereby a good deal of anger and conflict within the organization is presumably avoided.... This system of compensation assumes that the organization is a unit in which all members share in its success or failure. In terms of its compensation system, the *kaisha* is a more integrated and egalitarian organization than most companies in the West."[13]

With regard to the first point, no fat salaries, I had heard it so often that I tended to believe it. Much to my surprise, upon examining the evidence, it turned out that not even that statement was true. According to Towers Perrin, an international consulting firm known for its work on executive compensation, Japanese executives were not doing so poorly. In 1990, CEOs of major companies earned an average of $308,000, hardly a pittance. That was admittedly about half the American level. But it was exactly the same as CEOs in Great Britain and actually more than CEOs in Sweden, Holland and Spain.[14]

In making a case for a modest gap between executive and employee remuneration, Abegglen and Stalk quoted statistics from the Japan Federation of Employers Association (Nikkeiren), not necessarily the most unbiased source since it is a management lobby. According to these figures, the differential was about 8:1.[15] Other sources give similar figures, with *Toyo Keizai* finding a gap of 7:1 for listed companies, although the spread is probably greater in unlisted ones.[16] This is then loosely compared to the exorbitant incomes of certain American executives, the more exorbitant the better.

Such figures should be taken with a grain of salt. Perhaps a whole spoonfull to be on the safe side. First of all, the 8:1 gap is for after-tax compensation. Pre-tax it is about 15:1.

But that is only part of the problem. More essential is that most comparisons are between Japanese presidents and *newly recruited male college graduates*. Well, in the Japanese company hierarchy, that is hardly the bottom. These recruits are all fast-track employees expected one day to climb high in the organization. Fairer comparisons would have to be made between top executives and employees who are much further down. This can be done by referring back to the initial part of this section.

First, you can make a comparison with female college graduates, who are soon earning less than their male colleagues, and get a spread of about 10:1. Better yet, you can consider male high school graduates, just ordinary factory labor, and have something like 15:1. Or, why not try female high school graduates, which would perhaps result in 20:1. Of course, if you stick to the core company, the gap is artificially limited. If you bring in suppliers and subcontractors which are truly part of the extended company family, you are thinking in terms of gaps of anywhere from 30:1 and up. Finally, if you multiply by two for pre-tax earnings, you get 60:1.

The notion of equality becomes even more suspect when you recall that Japanese companies, to hide wage differentials and get around the tax laws routinely provide generous perks in lieu of wages. They are increasingly generous the further one rises in the hierarchy. While they are hard to convert into exact monetary terms, they probably add to the gap. For example, ordinary employees live in cramped dormitories or crummy company flats while executives have lovely detached houses. Ordinary employees are reimbursed for their commute to work, usually quite lengthy distances in crowded buses and subways. Executives have chauffeur-driven cars (a frill few Westerners get). Ordinary employees obviously have to pay for their own lunch and dinner. Senior staff seem to be eating almost all their meals at company expense, often in such luxurious restaurants and bars that an evening out costs more than an ordinary employee's total meal budget for the month. And they belong to golf clubs whose membership fee may be more than the average employee earns in a year.

Finally, and inevitably in the Japanese context, you must consider the little matter of prestige and status. Status is extremely important to Japanese, so much so that most would trade higher wages for higher status. Thus, being an executive, having the title, brings not only pride and satisfaction but honor and respect in a society where the pecking order is very strict and inferiors must play up to superiors more than in any Western society.

But there is one last dimension that must absolutely be drawn into the equation since it is subject to even more mythification than wages. That is the idea, propagated most firmly by Abegglen of late, that somehow the company (*kaisha*) belongs to its personnel.[17]

"The *kaisha* becomes in a real sense the property of the people who make it up. It will not be sold, in whole or in part, without specific approval of all its directors, acting on behalf of all its employees. Earnings of the company go first as a return to investors with the entire balance going to ensure the company's future and thus ensure the future of its employees."[18]

This notion that Japanese companies do not belong to their owners, indeed, that there are no "owners" as such, is very far-fetched if amazingly tenacious. Just to prove it wrong, it can be mentioned that there are millions of companies in Japan of which only several thousand are listed on the stock exchanges. The public companies are thus a tiny minority rather than the typical format, which is private. The private companies evidently belong to individuals, persons with names and authority. The public companies have broader ownership, often consisting of related or friendly firms, and sometimes even modest worker shareholding. Yet, many of the latter have been dominated and run by individuals as well.

The companies referred to are not minor ones. Private companies include many of the contractors, pharmaceutical firms, large wholesalers and retailers and even fair-sized manufacturers, such as YKK. Others, public in theory, were run by the founders or their family even after they ceased having significant shareholdings. They include, among many others, Bridgestone, Dai-ei, Honda, Matsushita, Kyocera, Seibu, Sony and the rest of the contractors, pharmaceutical firms, wholesalers, retailers, etc.

Not only did these "bosses" own and run the companies, they made imposing fortunes out of them. What they raked in each year, both through salaries and stock participations, could make the "exorbitant" pay packets of American executives look like petty cash. Quite a number became not only dollar millionaires but billionaires, including the world's two richest men: Taikichiro Mori (Mori) and Yoshiaki Tsutsumi (Seibu). Others who struck it rich were Konosuke Matsushita (National, Panasonic), Shoji Uehara (Taisho), Hiroshi Yamauchi (Nintendo), Makoto Iida (Secom), Kazuo Inamori (Kyocera), Tadao Yoshida (YKK), and many, many more. In such cases, the spread between the boss and ordinary employees could range from 100:1 to 1000:1 and more.

Which brings us to an extension of the "company belongs to its workers" thesis. That is that there are no class distinctions between workers and managers and there is no conflict between labor and capital such as embitters relations in Western companies. This view was emphatically, almost breathlessly expressed by another naive American academic, Professor Alan S. Blinder of Princeton. Just back from a brief stay, he revealed Japan's real "secret":

"The Japanese seem to have broken down the 'us vs. them'

Citizen Matsushita receiving homage from a worker.

Credit: Matsushita Electric

barriers that so often impair labor relations in American and European companies. They do so by creating a feeling that employees and managers share a common fate. To paraphrase Lincoln, a well-run Japanese corporation is of, by, and for its people.''[19]

Hoorah! Now we know what makes Japanese companies so successful!! Or, do we? As has been made amply clear, there are two groups in Japanese companies, there is an ''us'' and a ''them.'' The ''us'' is the ordinary workers, whether blue-collar or white-collar, male or female, old or young. The ''they'' is the management, whether paid managers, bureaucratic managers or the founders and their heirs. The interests of both groups are definitely not the same. They often disagree on how the company should be run and how any money should be spent. This is most acute with regard to labor's preference for shorter hours, better working conditions and higher wages, concerns which are most assuredly not shared by management.

There is also a second form of "us" and "them," namely the regulars who usually have better jobs, better pay, greater job security and higher status and the temporary or peripheral workers. And, finally, a third line can be drawn between those working for the parent company and those in the many subsidiaries, suppliers, subcontractors and others that revolve around it. In all three cases, as must already be evident, there are not only incipient class or social distinctions but a degree of "exploitation." Managers, regular employees, and parent companies can improve their own position by squeezing those who are dependent on them. This concept is rarely used in the literature on Japan, but it certainly deserves to be considered more often.

Birth Of An Aristocracy

It is one thing for money to be shuffled around, some getting richer, others poorer. It is quite another for classes to be created, with upper and lower burgeoning while the middle class shrivels. It is even more fateful when the better-off beget an aristocracy of sorts that can hand the gains down from generation to generation. That the first phenomenon has already occurred is plain to all. That the second and third, with much deeper social and political implications, are also coming to pass is not yet generally noticed.

This is extremely important in Japan because, along with equality, considerable stress is placed on meritocracy. The idea here, although it was probably always more *tatemae* than *honne,* is that family should not really count for that much in the economic and social advancement of individuals. They should rise—or fall—primarily through their own abilities, their willingness to work and sacrifice, and what they contribute to society. The key to meritocracy was education with the best students going furthest. This was basically an equality of opportunity which it was hoped would prevail.

One of the most obvious deviations has taken the form of transfers of wealth, while the parents are alive or after they pass away. These transfers are now substantial as can be seen from the inheritance figures which have been rising much faster than the general level of income. They totaled nearly ¥10 trillion a year by the late 1980s. By then, it was not unusual for parents to leave their children ¥10–20 million. But those who had really done well might bequeath billions. Kenji Osano, speculator and fixer *extraordinaire*, was rumored to have left behind ¥2–3 trillion. Konosuke Matsushita's personal fortune was evaluated at more than ¥350 billion.[20] Compared to this the estate of the late emperor was quite modest, a mere ¥2 billion. Admittedly, taxes ate up some of the money, but large amounts did pass from generation to generation spawning a growing coterie of well-to-do children and relatives.

Inheriting land also smooths the rise of many Japanese. Usually, these are not large chunks of land, but they can have incredibly large values on an overpriced market. It may seem odd to speak of a "landed aristocracy" consisting of heirs to plots that would seem puny anywhere else. In Japan, having or not having land is the main dividing line between the haves and the have-nots. For, those with land have a place to live and enhanced security. Alas, landholding is also becoming more concentrated with the land of the top fifth worth ten times more than that of the bottom fifth.[21]

This would not be so upsetting if education remained the prime path for advancement by the have-nots. Not so long ago, it still was. However, under the Japanese system, where it is necessary to get into proper feeder schools and prepare for exams in special classes, money is increasingly indispensable. The feeder schools and extra classes are very costly, more than the average family can afford. The average family can also not afford to send children to exclusive private colleges. So those less well off can only hope that their offspring will pass the tests for public colleges. Regrettably, according to recent surveys, more and more of the public college students come from the middle and upper classes.

That is doubly important. Good schooling is essential for anyone to rise in a society that places stress on education. But going to good schools, which is not quite the same thing, is crucial for one's social ascent. That is because the attempt at doing away with the elite school system has utterly failed. Even now, the bulk of those accepted as career bureaucrats come from top state universities, like Tokyo, Kyoto and others. The same applies to companies, which should theoretically pay more attention to business acumen, with the bulk of the presidents and higher executives coming from Tokyo, Kyoto or eminent private colleges like Waseda and Keio.[22]

More children are also "inheriting" their parents' professions. This is known as the second-generation boom (*nisei buumu*). Such practices are traditional for artists and artisans. But doctors are doing the same. They send their children to medical school, eventually make them partners, and ultimately leave them the clinic and clientele. The same occurs for dentists, accountants, lawyers, etc. That may be rather common in other countries. What is not is that ever more politicians have been handing their seats down to children and other relatives. This is becoming so widespread that "second-generation" Diet members now account for over a quarter of the total. Among them are the sons of former prime ministers Zenko Suzuki and Takeo Fukuda.

Of particular importance for the economy is that sons and other relatives or in-laws are increasingly rising to senior executive positions. This occurs not only in private companies, where the founders often own the company and can do as they want. It is making an appearance in listed ones that are supposedly based more on promotion by seniority and/or ability. Here, too, there are many examples, such as Tetsuo Goto of Tokyu Construction, Yoichi Tsuchiya of Sanyo Securities and Shinichiro Torii of Suntory. There are also the Hattoris of K. Hattori and Mogis of Kikkoman. While the links should be more tenuous, members of the Toyoda family have continued shaping the destiny of Toyota as have in-laws at Matsushita.

This shows that, although regarded as old-fashioned and not very admirable, nepotism remains strong. But it goes a big step further when parents decide who their children should marry and establish ties with other prominent families. In such instances, money can marry money, or political power, or social position. There are more and more of these marriages. Here are just some examples. Former prime minister Nakasone's daughter is married to the heir-apparent to Kajima Construction, Japan's largest contractor. Former prime minister Takeshita's youngest daughter is married to the son of the president of Takenaka Komuten, another big construction firm, and his oldest daughter is married to the son of another leading politician, Shin Kanemaru.

This is obviously creating a putative "elite," one which could in time become a new "aristocracy." Such an idea should definitely not be dismissed. This has happened in the past and can never be excluded in a society where family ties are so important and relations are still hierarchical. So, it is worthwhile considering who participates.

With wealth so significant, despite any feigned Confucian contempt, businessmen have clearly elevated their status. Those who head major companies enjoy broader acceptance, but the speculators can buy respectability as well. Ranking politicians in the ruling party are also members, since they do sort of run the country and many of them forged close links with business circles or became wealthy in their own right. Career bureaucrats, especially those who later entered the Diet or joined larger firms, are a third party.

It must be evident that the far-reaching sociological trends will have an impact on the economy. Much of the postwar ethos has been that individuals could rise through their own efforts. This injected a dynamism that had been lacking before and which was expressed in the founding of new companies, launching of new products and willingness to make sacrifices for one's own career. If that disappears, and it is impossible to go out on your own, to try out new ideas or even to rise in existing ventures, the economy would suffer. It would also be impaired if workers' sons felt they would remain workers or salarymen sensed that promotions would go to the relatives or friends of present executives. The existing gulf between labor and management would deepen notably if the latter were to become an elite that no longer cared about, or simply understood, the rank-and-file.

More broadly, if a new class or artistocracy is formed, its members will do their best to preserve whatever privileges they possess and gradually expand them. That would have serious macroeconomic implications, since one of the things they would surely want would be reduced taxation of wealth. By they way, they have already obtained more lenient inheritance taxes. That would not only cut down on the revenue available for public works and amenities, it would force the government to compensate elsewhere, probably by taxing companies or, much more likely, salaried workers and consumption. Although such policies would worsen the plight of the lower classes, it is unlikely that there would be any increase in welfare to help the neediest.

For those who remember the past, Japan has always been less generous and less enlightened under hereditary rulers or self-seeking elites who could ignore the mass of the population. It has also been less cooperative with foreigners and less amenable to criticism or influence. Finally, the leadership has frequently offered "bread and circuses" or foreign adventures as solutions to pressing domestic problems. It is therefore hard to imagine a scenario under which current trends could be deemed positive.

Notes

1. Akio Morita, *Made in Japan*, p. 149.
2. Economic Planning Agency, *White Paper on National Life*, 1988.
3. Prime Minister's Office, *Public Opinion Survey on the Life of the Nation*, 1990.
4. Nobuaki Takahashi, "Superpower Japan, the Closet Pauper," *Japan Echo*, Vol. XVI, 1989, p. 49.
5. See Albert J. Alletzhauser, *The House of Nomura*, and Robert Zielinski and Nigel Holloway, *Unequal Equities*.
6. *The Economist*, December 7, 1991.
7. See "Japan's Billionaires," *Tokyo Business Today*, October 1987, pp. 16–22.
8. See the *Forbes* and *Fortune* listings. In the 1991 listing, for example, there were 41 billionaires in Japan compared to 64 in the United States and 50 in Europe, both with populations twice as large. *Forbes*, July 8, 1991.
9. Over the past decades, land and stock speculators have repeatedly accounted for two-thirds to three-quarters of the hundred top taxpayers.
10. *The Economist*, April 28, 1991.
11. George Fields, "*Kakusa*—A New Buzzword Triggers Debate on Narrowing the Gap," *Tokyo Business Today*, January 1989, p. 25.
12. Ministry of Labor, *Basic Survey on Wage Structure*.
13. James Abegglen and George Stalk, Jr., *Kaisha*, p. 198.
14. TPF&C, *1990 Executive Pay Update*. This survey covered CEOs in large companies ($250 million annual sales) in twenty countries. Of these, Japan was actually tied for eighth place with regard to total remuneration (cash, benefits, perquisites and long-term incentives).
15. Abegglen and Stalk, op. cit., p. 192.
16. *Tokyo Business Today*, December 1991, p. 58.
17. While Abegglen does not explain where his ideas came from, this *kaisha-*

ism bears a striking resemblance to the *kigyoism* (using another word for corporation) which was floated by Japanese bureaucrats and managers. The most complete description can be found in a book by an ex-MITI man Koji Matsumoto, *The Rise of the Japanese Corporate System.*

18. Abegglen and Stalk, op. cit., p. 207.
19. Allan S. Blinder, "How Japan Puts the 'Human' in Human Capital," *Business Week,* November 11, 1991, p. 22.
20. *Mainichi,* April 27, 1989.
21. *Wall Street Journal,* June 20, 1989.
22. These four colleges presently account for 45 percent of all presidents of companies listed on the first section of the stock exchange. *Tokyo Business Today,* December 1991, p. 58.

11
The Crisis Cometh

So Far, No Good

There is an odd intellectual conceit that, when one criticizes the Japanese economy, the heavy burden of proof is on the critic. Why, I may be asked, have you written so many nasty things about Japan? In theory, that is nonsense. Any economy, even the most perfect, has flaws. In practice, it is even sillier. When an economy has been weakening and fails to provide much material or spiritual well-being, as is Japan's situation, the onus should lie with those who claim it is exceptional to prove their case.

Still, I have no objection to summing up the various charges. Nor do I hesitate to explain why I am so critical. The essence is really quite simple. I am critical because there is a lot to be critical about!

First of all, growth, Japan's strongest claim to superiority. That is a thing of the past. As noted, the economy has not been particularly vigorous nor managed to maintain a semblance of its earlier strength except in some few respects. Overall growth rates have slipped sharply, from more than 10 percent to less than 5 percent, the magic figure its supporters once regarded as low beyond belief. This growth, as also mentioned, is grotesquely lopsided. Relatively few branches are strong and productive; quite a few are amazingly weak and wasteful.

Japanese economic management, contrary to the general impression, has not been especially brilliant. Planning was rather superficial, if not whimsical, and monetary and fiscal policies have often backfired. Inflation, while extremely low in theory, surely underestimated the level given the incredible run-up in asset values. The same applied to unemployment, far greater than conceded by official sources.

The one relative success in this field has been targeting. There is no question but that the bureaucrats and businessmen accelerated the emergence of certain sectors, hastened the expansion of production and strengthened the position of key players. That was certainly helpful while it lasted. Now, however, there are considerably fewer new products to target. Instead, bureaucrats and businessmen are banding together to rescue or ease the decline of sectors that, officially at least, the Japanese regard as no longer worthy. And this at great cost. In fact, the Japanese are not much better than other advanced countries on this count.

Still, and this is also to the good, Japanese companies have grown very competitive, some of them at least. They produce high quality articles cheaply and efficiently. They can export them widely. And they constantly expand their market share at home and abroad. On the other hand, to do so, they occasionally form groups or cartels that keep prices artificially high for Japanese consumers and reduce them enough to undercut foreign competitors. Fine for the companies, not so great for the consumers and foreigners.

So much for the outright, or relatively positive, aspects. They can be admired, if you will. The rub is that this has not done much to improve the lives of ordinary Japanese. The economy has occasionally been quite productive; it has rarely been very fruitful. People continue to endure living standards that are much poorer than would be expected of a country with such a large gross domestic product and such high personal incomes. Housing is rather mediocre, amenities are lacking, even consumer goods are not that abundant. Yet, nobody has worked harder to achieve material gains than the Japanese.

More broadly, life is rather constricted. There is little leisure, little time for one's family, little time for oneself. Neighborhood life has suffered. So has national life. The quality of life is perfectly inadequate, much lower than in equally advanced countries. But even the quality of working life, supposedly a Japanese specialty, leaves much to be desired. Meanwhile, economic and social gaps are growing between the haves and have-nots, the new rich and the new poor, with the rising elite and nascent aristocracy grabbing more than they deserve.

The overwhelming concern, however, is not that ordinary people have gained insufficiently from growth, production and competitiveness but that they are worried about the future. The health and welfare schemes have not been adequately funded, certainly not given the enormous demands that can be expected by the next century. Nor are there the facilities and personnel needed to ease the declining years of the population. With the number of aged growing so rapidly, and the contingents of younger people thinning, there is valid cause for anxiety.

This is a very mixed review. Some good, some bad. The key, as was indicated in the introduction, is not how many aspects are good or bad but how significant they are and to whom. Perhaps to bureaucrats, businessmen and economists, economic production and competitiveness are all-important. For the vast majority of just plain folks, what they get out of the economy counts more. And what the Japanese obtain is precious little compared to what they put in.

Is this enough to speak of a crisis? Well, yes and no. The situation has been reasonably pleasant for high tech sectors and remarkably congenial for those who possessed land, stocks or companies. But it has been rather depressing for sectors like shipbuilding, shipping, textiles and garments, and even worse for mining and fishing. Peripheral workers, most notably those in peripheral companies, have had trouble making ends meet. Even the archetypical salaryman is feeling the pinch. This is most noticeable for those who cannot afford a home or have to live in more remote suburbs. As for the elderly, the life of those without large pensions, substantial savings or children to fall back on is becoming miserly and miserable.

Certainly, if not yet a full-blown crisis, this is a (coming) crisis. For this worsening of the economy and the well-being of many people took place with a growth rate that was still quite decent. What would happen if that rate were to slip further, as can be expected? Then there would be a marked deterioration of the situation. Anyway, most Japanese are getting tired of plugging away under an economic regime that gives so little in return. To them, it seems more like an endless treadmill where you must walk faster and faster just to stand still. And they are frightened out of their wits about what might happen if they were to slow down.

In this light, one might consider some other countries whose economic system is admittedly not as dynamic or powerful as Japan's. Yet, they have obtained more for their workers and the populace in general. What is especially intriguing about these comparisons is that they are supposedly afflicted by an economic crisis while Japan, in the eyes of many, is not.

True, the German economy has not grown as rapidly as the Japanese. But it has expanded very considerably since war's end. German income is not much lower than Japanese levels . . . on paper. When it comes to purchasing power, there is no doubt that Germans can buy much more and boast vastly greater affluence. They also live in larger, more solid houses, closer to town. They have more amenities, attractive neighborhoods and considerable leisure. The quality of life is much finer and German workers, unlike the Japanese, actually do participate in shaping working conditions. To round things out, social security and welfare are more extensive.

This is not accidental. The German people, trade unions, government and business community have sought (or accepted) more balanced development. They have traded slower growth for more leisure, more amenities, more environmental protection. They have not allowed companies to rip off consumers as brazenly and, when they export, they get something for it. Thus, profitability is higher and prosperity greater, even without an obsession with competitiveness. What applies to Germany, by the way, applies in differing degrees to much of Europe, with Sweden, Switzerland, Holland, France, even Great Britain and Italy having a more fruitful if less productive economy.

No need to stop here. Japan has long ceased being a growth hero. Its economy was bound to slow down after two decades of rapid growth, the apologists say. Well, the economies of Korea, Taiwan, Hong Kong and Singapore have been growing more swiftly for well over twenty years and show no sign of flagging. They are even more competitive for certain products and export proportionately more, much more, than Japan. In fact, they have been eating into Japan's market share around the world and are the biggest threat to its economic and export growth.

Yet, there is some balance. While working very long hours, most other East Asians have not sold their soul to the company. Free time is theirs to use as they see fit, whether with friends or the family, which remains intact. Despite sometimes regimented societies, the state has usually provided more public housing and better amenities given the relative economic situation. Companies, especially those in the Chinese communities, have achieved far greater profitability

and more of this seeped down into the populace, where workers could create their own companies and advance without
being stymied by cartels. Consumers, always on the lookout
for a bargain, also got more for their money even if the
consumer was not theoretically God.

This may not impress the Japanese. They seem to live in
a simplified world consisting of only two countries, Japan
and the United States. America's failure is *ipso facto* Japan's
"success." Unfortunately, as ever, the Japanese establishment is using its own yardstick. True, economic growth is
sluggish, companies are less competitive, Japanese interlo-
pers are boosting exports and controling more of the U.S.
market. Still, on the whole, the average American leads a
more comfortable and relaxed life than the average Japanese.
So, there must be something wrong somewhere!

Why then this awe of the Japanese economy? Why must
a critic justify every swipe he makes at that economy? The
evidence is crystal clear. The Japanese economy is grossly
unbalanced, it is not very fruitful, it does not produce what
the people want, and it is not even growing very rapidly
anymore. Elsewhere, in supposedly inferior economies,
things are not all that bad and, despite any complaints, people
surely live better. I rest my case.

What About The Future?

As we all know, it is easier to forecast the past than the
future, although most Japanapologists have done a crummy
job even with the former. When it comes to the future, the
Japan claque again expects it to outperform the rest and continue its hypothetical economic "miracle." Again, I disagree.
But much of this argument must be based less on facts—
which do not yet exist—than educated guesses and hunches.

Part of it, however, has a pretty solid basis. For example,
it is fairly safe to maintain that the situation for amenities

will not improve much. After all, with land accounting for most of the total cost of each public works project, no country would be rich enough to greatly improve the network. Similarly, for social security and welfare, the amounts of money that will be needed are so vast that not even the richest country could come up with them. In addition, if economic growth does slow down, tax revenue will grow more sluggishly and the ability to fund amenities, education, health, social security or anything else will decrease.

So the crux, once again, is growth. Now, much more than before, there is good reason to doubt another burst of speed. The economy has matured further. In manufacturing, there are fewer futuristic sectors than ever, most of those presently known having already been exploited, and those lying beyond the horizon remaining very uncertain and costly to develop. At the same time, the number of mature sectors, to say nothing of declining ones, has increased substantially. It is really hard to divine where the desired growth can come from. The Japanese are counting on the "ABCD Industries" or automation, biotechnology, computers and data processing to do the trick. But they will probably need the whole alphabet.

The principal cause of concern is that, for the first time in its history, Japan is not a follower but a pathbreaker. It can no longer simply borrow existing products, made with existing technologies, and sell them on existing markets. It is necessary to create new products, technologies and markets. That calls for a degree of creativity that has not been found locally. Even buying up foreign venture capital firms or tapping into foreign research institutes will not be enough. A radical change in the attitudes not only of researchers but managers is called for and there is little sign that it is emerging.

Services, on the other hand, still have plenty of room both for growth and enhanced efficiency. The possibilities exist and the money is there to develop them. But this may again be impeded by social constraints, including the excessive craving for service and profligate use of personnel. Construction and farming could also become considerably more productive, assuming the political support (and subsidies) were withdrawn. For all of this, however, it would be critical for consumers to insist on getting a fairer deal. As long as they put service ahead of cost, and allow protection and subsidization, there is no motivation to rationalize.

Some of the greatest threats to growth are external. The economy has long been export-led and, despite repeated attempts at converting, it remains so today. That is partly because Japanese products are excellent and foreign consumers like them. It is also because they are sold aggressively, often cross-subsidized, sometimes dumped. Foreign trading partners have repeatedly complained about this. Occasionally, they have reacted, imposing special duties, tariffs or other restrictions or forcing the Japanese to exercise retraint. But their patience may be wearing thin and, even if it is not, they simply cannot afford to continue running huge trade deficits. This reduces the chances of expanding trade and increases the likelihood of managed trade, protectionism and an all-out trade war.

Many of these problems could be avoided if, rather than pressing for exports, Japan were to further develop the domestic economy, which sorely needs it. It could obtain the financial resources if, instead of pushing for market share, companies were to seek profits. Both of these policies are feasible. After all, they prevail in most other countries. Foreign partners would not be upset. If anything, they would be relieved. Indeed, they have been urging such reforms on Japan for years.

So much for the "hard" aspects. What about the softer, human aspects which may prove more decisive? That is actually the greater source of worries. As noted, the younger generations which are expected to run the economy in the future are markedly different from the older generations that have been in charge thus far. Youngsters are less willing to work, less willing to sacrifice, less willing to cooperate. They have the skills, and sometimes the ambition, but they do not really fancy the present economic mechanism. They do not believe in all work and no play nor in working hard to obtain relatively little.

Unlike their elders, many younger Japanese know what is wrong and would gladly mend the system to make it more fruitful and humane. But, unlike their elders, they do not hold the levers of control. They may eventually do so one day. However, after having risen ever so slowly to the top, and being selected for posts of leadership because they were obedient followers, they may not have the will to impose change either. Whether they can continue as dynamically as their predecessors, many of them genuine entrepreneurs, is most uncertain and so far the novice executives have been of indifferent caliber.

Lastly, there are two factors that are particularly ominous but will be impossible to avoid. One is that Japanese workers, even if they were to maintain an acceptable work ethic, will be among the most expensive in the world. Wages are already higher than in many advanced countries, five times as high as in newly industrialized countries, and ten times the level of true developing countries. Secondly, even if they earn their keep, there may simply not be enough workers given the plummeting birth rate. Many companies will disappear for want of successors and others will find it hard to expand. This shortage, by the way, will come at a very difficult time for the social security system, with fewer workers carrying more pensioners.

While these trends can be readily discerned and their implications fathomed, an accentuated economic and social polarization could be even more disruptive but in still uncertain ways. It seems probable that the rich will continue getting richer and the poor, poorer. After all, the former have accumulated most of the assets. They can also enhance their status and power. The rest of the population may not accept this gladly given the remnants of an egalitarian ethos. And, if there is no longer as much to be gained by studying harder, working harder or striving for advancement, they may either cease such efforts or turn against the system.

To sum things up, I do not doubt that the Japanese economy can continue growing, probably somewhat faster than other advanced countries. It may even become the world's biggest economy in terms of gross domestic product by the turn of the century. Its companies will be larger, tougher and more formidable competitors than ever, quite capable of clobbering foreign rivals. And, unless obstructed by external pressure or barriers, they will export more goods than they allow into Japan.

But, and this is an extremely big BUT, such achievements will mean little to anyone but statisticians. For the Japanese people will still not boast a real income (i.e. what they can actually buy), living environment or quality of life that compares favorably to their peers. Nor will they have much in the way of leisure or security in old age. For them, the economic "miracle" will be a tantalizing yet elusive "mirage."

Rising, Setting Or Immobile?

If there is one factor which, more than any other, militates for a sorry end to Japan's "miraculous" economy, then it is the inability to adapt rapidly enough and undertake essential reforms even when they are broadly perceived as indispensable. Of course, here too it is useful to separate *tatemae* from *honne* and discard all sorts of spurious events which, at the time, look like movement and change but gradually dissipate. It is also helpful to discount comments from well-meaning observers, like Bill Emmott of *The Economist*, who emphatically insisted: "There is one foreign myth that is worse than all the rest. It is that Japan does not change or, expressed more mildly, that it is especially resistant to change."[1]

To prove his point, after years of giving news the now familiar *Economist* slant, he wrote a book entitled *The Sun Also Sets*. One might naively assume that it would portray the decay and decline of the Japanese economy. Instead, it forecast an admirable maturation and fulfillment with the Japanese system turning into something more like ours. People would work less and earn more, they would begin to enjoy life, companies would not export as aggressively, in fact, imports would rise more appreciably and trade would be balanced. In short, it assumed that the Maekawa plan was actually being implemented when it was nothing more than window-dressing.

Unsurprisingly the book was popular not only with the general public, which thought it was truly a critical work, but the Japanese authorities who knew it was not. After all, it pictured exactly the sort of Japan they had been promising for years and wanted foreigners to think was really on the way. Like so many other foreign journalists, Emmott obliged. Just like the rest of them, he was wrong. His image of a brave new world was shattered in no time. Imports expanded briefly, more as a result of the heavy yen than anything else. By 1991 already, any improvement ceased and Japan's export surplus rebounded. While some Japanese had windfall profits they could spend, many more were worse off because of higher housing and other costs. Leisure was not much greater and old age security more distant than ever.

Admittedly, things were going on all the time. There was deregulation of banks, securities firms and certain protected industries. More nontariff barriers were removed and impediments to distribution relaxed. Lots of money was made, lots of money was spent. Luxuries became so widespread that they were absolutely commonplace. But things happening is not change, it is just changes. CHANGE is something more conscious, more purposeful, hopefully more beneficial.

That change has come so slowly to Japan puzzles the Japanese, and gullible foreigners, who believe one of the hoariest myths. We Japanese are slow to decide, it runs, but once we decide we move ahead ruthlessly. You foreigners, in contrast, decide quickly. But you are slow to implement. This sort of observation sounds particularly silly on the background of recent decades which witnessed Reaganism in America, Thatcherism in Great Britain, *glasnost* and *perestroika* in the Soviet Union, the fall of communism in the East and return of capitalism there and in Latin America. All this while, it is only Japan which has escaped wide-ranging change.

Why is change so slow in Japan. Can it come at all? I do not endorse the extreme view, namely that Japan cannot change. It can, and does, and will. But this change is tortuous. Why? I also do not subscribe to the idea that the problems lies in a "system" which was described by Karel Van Wolferen as a web without a spider, a circle of counterveiling forces with nobody in control.[2] He knows much more about Japan than Emmott, he knows more about Japan than I do, but that answer is too pat. I prefer a more traditional analysis. According to it, to foreshadow the answer, change is slow and tortuous because it is resisted by those forces for their own reasons.

Which are the groups seeking change? The people on the whole, especially as workers (shorter hours), consumers (lower prices) and taxpayers (less waste). There is some support from small businesses, to avoid domination by big companies, but shopkeepers, tradesmen and farmers want to keep their own petty privileges. Young people are certainly more eager for change than the old, but elderly folks surely do want better security and welfare provisions. Women are sometimes more subversive than men, since the situation satisfies them less. Putting it all together, you have the vast majority of the population that desires change. But these are all, as we have seen, quite weak and disorganized sectors.

The other proponent of change, only slightly more focused, is external. It consists of Japan's allies and trading partners, which want the economy liberalized and the export-orientation dulled so that their own businessmen stand a chance. They also want Japan to share the burden of defense, aid and general economic stability. Since they are important politically, and could hurt the economy as well, Japan must listen. This is especially true for larger players, like the United States and European Community. But the impact of *gaiatsu* or foreign pressure should not be exaggerated, for the Japanese establishment is a master at accepting formally and evading informally.

Those who defend the *status quo,* and resist change, the "spider" in short, are a much tighter coalition of big business, the ruling party and career bureaucrats. More specifically, it consists of their higher echelons which are male, elderly, conservative and elitist. There is no question whatsoever that they control the economy as well as the state machinery. They impose the measures they want and oppose the rest, whether or not they are endorsed by the people. Japan's questionable "democracy" is such that they can get away with it most of the time even if they have to offer a sop now and then.

Like all elites, the clique running Japan tends to mistake its own advantages for those of the system and assume that the system should be maintained even if people down below complain. Thus, while workers gripe about overtime, managers are delighted with the practice. While citizens grump about taxes, the bureaucrats are quite pleased. And the ruling politicians love an arrangement that offers perpetual power. Moreover, in their eyes, the economy is a success. It has brought growth and competitiveness and that is all they regard as important. Any failings are secondary. Meanwhile, they are told by foreign sycophants just how successful they were. Why, they ask themselves, tamper with a good thing?

Aside from that, change is impeded by certain quirks of the "typical" decision-making mechanisms. We have all heard that it takes a long time for the Japanese to reach decisions. Long is an understatement. It takes almost forever because they are based on consensus, which is much harder to achieve (and preserve) than a mere majority. Everybody has to be heard out, perhaps offered some counterpart, and brought in. Everybody, that is, who counts. To satisfy all, any decision is usually loose and vague and can be understood in many different ways.

This bring us to implementation, which is supposedly swift once the decision has been reached. Still, it is hard to grasp why a decision that is ambiguous, consisting of awkward compromises and open to variable interpretations should be easy to apply. In practice, it is not. It has to be repeatedly adjusted and corrected, this taking time. Moreover, one decision on any subject is rarely enough. Each step in the long march to implementation calls for its own decision-making meetings and *nemawashi*, which can drag on and on.

Oddly enough, the more urgent change becomes, the harder it is to obtain. The Japanese do not like quick decisions, they need plenty of time for personal contacts and "root-binding." In a crisis, they are terribly afraid that their constituency will lose more than it gains and they dig their heels in. Pressure, whether domestically or from abroad, only aggravates things. Thus, when the economy is declining or weakening it is actually harder to take action than when it is doing fairly well and there is no great rush. So, the best opportunities are often missed and the worst create deadlocks.

Nowadays, decision-making and change are even slower for another reason. Those who are in positions of authority are much older. The once eager young bureaucrats, dynamic entrepreneurs and budding politicians have grown very old and tired, and some have stepped down. Alas, they were not replaced by young men but others almost their age. The average age of the leadership is now in the sixties, sometimes seventies, with youngsters of forty or fifty quite the exception. It is extremely hard to get such people to agree on anything, but change is hardest of all. For, to some extent at least, it implies disapproval of what they or their predecessors did. And they are so far removed from the younger generations that they scarcely know what is wanted.

These factors have repeatedly combined to sap or frustrate attempts at reform. Thus, despite the crying need and the sustained demands, nothing much came of the educational, fiscal, administrative or political reform movements. Equality for women was scuttled. While realizing that younger workers had to be handled differently, little was done to reshape the management system to provide more opportunity. Instead, the core of regular workers was reduced and the most loyal were worked harder, sometimes to death.

The most obvious failure occurred for the Maekawa plan or, more accurately, the exchange rate appreciation imposed on Japan. The idea was that Japanese goods would cost more and imported (especially American) goods less, thereby improving the trade balance. Japanese companies could ride this out by raising prices to maintain margins and the economy could hold up by switching to domestic demand. Instead, in a state of near panic, manufacturers rationalized, cut costs and were able to export as much as before at the new rate.

To do so, they squeezed margins, kept wage increases down, and laid off workers. A lot of good it did them. With export-oriented growth resumed, there were renewed complaints and renewed threats from abroad and growing chances of yet another *endaka* crisis.

This means that change is more likely to come in one of two ways, neither particularly desirable. The first, which has occurred periodically in the past, is allowing external factors or foreign powers to engineer change, peacefully or otherwise. This happened under the influence of ancient China, with the arrival of Perry's "black ships," with defeat in the Pacific War and, in smaller measure, through pressure to open the market and deregulate the economy. However, on a relatively peaceful, stable and civilized world scene, this source will be minor and incremental.

That being so, this time change is liable to come from within. But probably not smoothly or constructively. Despite the rigidity of the system, there is some room for inputs from below. Younger salarymen can initiate *ringisho* and hope that, in due course and perhaps much modified, their proposals will be approved by their superiors. Factory workers can at least put a suggestion in the box. There are not even as many formal channels in the bureaucracies, political parties and other social institutions. But at least younger members can float ideas, especially the college-educated males who are expected to take over one day. Far less scope is offered to females and almost none to those who are not full members, such as temporary or part-time workers, opposition politicians or trade unionists.

Since the populace does not have many formal means of modifying the *status quo*, the alternatives are not very propitious. During the 1950s, workers held demonstrations and strikes, sometimes quite violent ones, to defend their rights. There were broad anti-conservative coalitions, occasionally turning into antiwar and anti-American movements. Then came student radicals in the 1960s. But most of the open, shrill protests have long since disappeared and the population seems to accept the existing order, on the surface at least. Indeed, superficial observers might wonder whether this is not quite a contented society.

Underneath, however, there is incessant movement. As noted, the younger generations hold views that are not only very different from their elders, they are absolutely subversive when compared to traditional values. And younger people do follow them. Dissatisfied workers cannot impose shorter hours or more pay, but they can move to other companies that offer them or slack off. Women increasingly go their way. If they cannot pursue a career, they will seek other outlets for their energy. While appearing to participate in social activities and making the right motions, citizens will often shirk their responsibilities.

This means that the foundation for Japan's heavy and rigid superstructure has been rotting away. There is almost no political participation, aside from voting. Company employees are ever less willing to sacrifice for the *kaisha*'s benefit. Women hesitate to found a family and bring up kids, which deprives society of its lifeblood. Education has become a drag, work a bore and organized society an imposition many youngsters try to avoid. While the Japanese often look down on other countries as inferior, that is usually the extent of their patriotism.

Down below, there is considerable anger and frustration. But it is contained. Or it has been sublimated into various forms of cheap and futile pleasure-seeking. That is hardly likely to result in an explosion. But a society—and an economy—can be severely impaired and even destroyed by a continuing implosion as one erstwhile pillar after the other crumbles. That, too, will bring change. Alas, it will hardly be conscious, purposeful or beneficial.

The sun may yet set on the Japanese economy. As we

saw, it has already ceased rising as vigorously as before and may be approaching its zenith with regard to growth. With regard to everything else, everything that makes an economy worthwhile, like more pay, leisure, quality of life, security, it has probably begun to decline. Unless Japan does change, or at least reverse some of the existing trends, it should continue sinking to the point that even the apologists will have to admit that a crisis is coming . . . if not already here.

Crime And Punishment

Once again, it should not be assumed that these dark thoughts, these sour notes, come solely from foreign critics like myself. Every comment here has been stated and echoed many times over by the Japanese themselves. At the risk of further boring readers, let it be noted that they are also reflected in the opinion polls.

On the most general level, what do the Japanese expect of the future? Well, judging by comments, writings and polls, they are not acutely worried, there is no panic or deep anxiety in the body politic, although it surely exists for many individuals. On the other hand, there is hardly a mood of optimism or an underlying feeling that, come what may, the Japanese economy will not only get by but do so with flying colors. Moreover, the clear trend has been for the optimists to decrease and the pessimists to increase over recent years. The further out the future is placed, the less convinced people are that things will turn out well.

This was shown by the results over time of the Public Opinion Survey on the Life of the Nation. When asked whether their lives had improved over the past year, only 11 percent responded affirmatively in 1990 as opposed to about 25 percent until the 1973 oil crisis. Somewhat more, 14 percent, indicated that their lives had become worse. When it came to future prospects, 23 percent expected improvement and only 11 percent that things would get worse. But, again, prior to 1973, those with positive expectations accounted for over 30 percent. Most interestingly, when asked whether today's children would enjoy better lives than today's adults, 26 percent thought life would be harder versus 26 percent who thought it would be easier with the negative camp growing most rapidly.[3]

Another public opinion survey by the Prime Minister's Office, this time on "society and state," asked where Japan was moving in a good or bad direction. The highest positive ranking, but with only 52 percent support, was economic power. Welfare only garnered 24 percent, down significantly over the years. Figures for negative trends were much higher, showing 30 percent for the social situation, 43 percent for land and housing and 61 percent for natural environment.[4]

Dissatisfaction is also shown in the media, where criticisms as severe as any in this book can be found every day. Just to let readers know what local journalists think of the situation, and the government's efforts, I am quoting the latest editorial from *Nihon Keizai Shimbun,* Japan's leading financial newspaper. Even harsher remarks come from mainstream monthly and weekly magazines and more anti-establishment papers. But this is quite adequate to get the drift.

"Business confidence in Japan has been deteriorating at a rate almost on a par with the bewildering pace of the disintegration of the Soviet Union. The sharp downturn in industry was amply demonstrated in the Bank of Japan's quarterly economic outlook survey. . . . All these business barometers point to the need for timely policy initiatives from the government, whose perception of the present situation appears curiously out of tune with that of the private sector. Business circles are widely pessimistic about the future. . . . Maintaining a reasonable level of growth, therefore, remains a goal that the Japanese government should make every effort to achieve. Frankly, what the government has been doing makes one wonder whether it is sufficiently serious in its concern over the country's economic health."[5]

Japanese academics have had equally unpleasant things to say about the economic situation. Actually, they have engaged in rather far-reaching criticism. But, as a last example, I prefer quoting a bureaucrat, Nobuaki Takahashi, who could hardly be accused of Japan-bashing. He has worked for MITI, one of the think tanks and now the Japan Development Bank. Yet, his comments strike many notes that reverberate from this book.

"Japan's postwar economic growth has given rise to two myths. The first is that the rate and duration of Japan's growth has no parallel anywhere else in the world; the second is that this continuation of growth will necessarily lead to affluence for the Japanese people. But other nearby countries are now surging forward as rapidly as Japan once did, and true affluence has yet to be realized by the Japanese even after more than 40 years of economic expansion.

"Any country that picks the right model, mimics that model's production technology, and has an industrious work force capable of assimilating what it learns ought to be able to achieve high-level economic development. Yet if this country aims only at elevating industrial efficiency and building up production capacity, it may foster thriving businesses and accumulate national wealth, but it will not be able to give its people a high standard of living. When we realize that this is the road Japan has followed, our faith in a growth-first policy is shaken.

"Many people are angry that the money they have toiled to earn is not making their lives richer. It is being siphoned off by high prices for farm products and services sheltered from foreign competition and by exorbitant rates and commissions in protectively regulated transportation, communications, and financial markets. Much of it passes through a real estate market where lunacy reigns and winds up in the hands of a small group of investors and businesses."[6]

It probably matters less that the population, media and enlightened critics are increasingly concerned about the future than that the elite is getting worried. This could be noted both from statements of intention and agitation for reform. In fact, over the past decade, suggestions for reform have come fast and furious and some were tentatively introduced. This included fiscal, financial and administrative reform, educational, social and welfare reform, even political reform. There was also talk of the need to revamp the management system, playing down seniority and enhancing opportunities for younger, more individualistic employees.

That something, and something fairly radical, had to be done was occasionally perceived even at the top. The most comprehensive view involved a restructuring of the economy. The work was initiated by Prime Minister Nakasone, back in the mid–1980s, and many senior bureaucrats and businessmen approved. This resulted in the Maekawa plan and its successors. While the stress was on more balanced trade and growth arising more from domestic demand, there was also a recognition of the need for more amenities and social infrastructure, greater social security and welfare, and a "revolutionary improvement in the quality of life."

That is why I have never considered it a "crime" to criticize Japan. It is not even criminal when the accusations are strong and the language harsh. For they are justified by the facts. Claiming that all is well, that Japan's economy is in great shape, and that the Japanese are satisfied with the situation, is actually more criminal. It does not run contrary to any law I know. But it is a crime against the truth. And it is

particularly impermissible when committed by foreign journalists and academics whose responsibility it is to seek and
convey the truth.

Yet, despite the fact that the economic situation is considerably worse now than a decade ago, the bulk of the
media commentary and learned literature ignores the evidence. The supposed "experts" do not bother showing the
weaknesses and failings. Some do not seem aware that any
exist. Others try to explain them away or justify them. That
there is no shortage of apologists was demonstrated by the
ease in collecting silly statements for inclusion in this book.

How can the Japanapologists be stopped? I don't rightly
know. Apparently, you cannot lock people up for telling
lies. You cannot confound them in open debate because
they refuse to communicate with those who disagree. You
cannot remove them from the editorial boards of publications
or departments of Japanese studies for reasons of ignorance
and incompetence, that is too widespread. Anyway, they
control appointments. All that remains is to make them look
foolish.

That explains why, in all my books, I have made reference
to some of the ludicrous statements that circulate. It has not
been hard to find them, there are so many. And they are so
easily disproven. While I would sorely miss this element of
levity in books that might otherwise be too somber, I would
forgo it if only we could stop the misinformation. Then, and
it would be a relief, we could have truly worthwhile and
constructive discussions.

There is, however, one other possibility. It was suggested
to me by the words of the Lord High Executioner in Gilbert
and Sullivan's *Mikado,* a more accurate portrayal of Japan
than some recent bestsellers. We really should "make the
punishment fit the crime." The most fitting punishment for
foreigners praising a system that is not even liked by the
locals is to make them live under it. The Japanapologists

should all be packed off to Japan, to live there like ordinary Japanese and not exalted *gaijin*. Under those conditions, it would not take long for them to repent. In the meantime, I am certain, they would provide us with a source "of innocent merriment, OF INNOCENT MERRIMENT."

NOTES

1. Bill Emmott, *The Sun Also Sets*, p. 28.
2. Karel van Wolferen, *The Enigma of Japanese Power*.
3. Prime Minister's Office, *Public Opinion Survey on the Life of the Nation*, 1990.
4. Prime Minister's Office, *Public Opinion Survey on Society and State*, 1991.
5. *Nikkei Weekly*, December 28, 1991.
6. Nobuaki Takahashi, "Superpower Japan, the Closet Pauper," *Japan Echo*, Vol. XVI, 1989, pp. 47–51.

Bibliography

1. Economic
2. Management
3. Industrial Relations
4. Women Workers
5. Cultural, Social, Political

1. Economic

Czinkota, Michael R., and Woronoff, Jon, *Unlocking Japan's Market*, Chicago, Probus, London, Pitman, 1991.

Dodwell Marketing Consultants, *Industrial Groupings in Japan*, Tokyo, 1990.

Emmott, Bill, *The Sun Also Sets*, New York, Random House, 1988.

Gibney, Frank, *Miracle by Design, The Real Reasons Behind Japan's Economic Success*, New York, Times Books, 1982.

Inoguchi, Takashi, and Okimoto, Daniel I., *The Political Economy of Japan: The Changing International Context*, Stanford, Stanford University Press, 1988.

Kahn, Herman, *The Emerging Japanese Superstate*, Harmondsworth, Penguin, 1970.

Kosai, Yutaka, *The Era of High-Speed Growth*, Tokyo, University of Tokyo Press, 1986.

Lincoln, Edward J., *Japan, Facing Economic Maturity*, Washington, Brookings Institution, 1988.

———, *Japan's Unequal Trade*, Washington, Brookings Institution, 1990.

Morris-Suzuki, T., and Seiyama, T. (eds.), *Japanese Capitalism Since 1945*, Armonk, M. E. Sharpe, 1989.

Nakamura, Takafusa, *The Postwar Japanese Economy*, Tokyo, University of Tokyo Press, 1981.
Nester, William R., *Japanese Industrial Targeting*, London, Macmillan, 1990.
Shinohara, Myohei, *Industrial Growth, Trade and Dynamic Patterns in the Japanese Economy*, Tokyo, Tokyo University Press, 1982.
Uchino, Tatsuro, *Japan's Postwar Economy*, Tokyo, Kodansha International, 1983.
Van Der Meer, Cornelius L.J., and Yamada, Saburo, *Japanese Agriculture*, London, Routledge, 1990.
Vogel, Ezra, *Comeback*, New York, Simon & Schuster, 1985.
Woronoff, Jon, *Japanese Targeting, Successes, Failures, Lessons*, London, Macmillan, and New York, St. Martin's, 1992.
——, *Japan's Commercial Empire*, London, Macmillan, and Armonk, M.E. Sharpe, 1984.
——, *Japan's Management Mystique*, Chicago, Probus, 1992.
——, *The Japan Syndrome*, New Brunswick, Transaction Books, 1985.
——, *World Trade War*, New York, Praeger, 1984.
Yamamura, Kozo, *Economic Policy in Postwar Japan: Growth versus Economic Democracy*, Seattle, University of Washington Press, 1967.
——, and Yasuba, Yasukichi, *The Political Economy of Japan: The Domestic Transformation*, Stanford, Stanford University Press, 1987.
Zielinski, Robert, and Holloway, Nigel, *Unequal Equities*, Tokyo, Kodansha International, 1990.

2. Management

Abegglen, James C., and Stalk, George, Jr., *Kaisha, The Japanese Corporation*, New York, Basic Books, 1985.
Arai, Shunzo, *An Intersection of East and West, Japanese Business Management*, Tokyo, Rikugei, 1971.
Hayashi, Shuji, *Culture and Management in Japan*, Tokyo, University of Tokyo Press, 1989.
Matsumoto, Koji, *The Rise of The Japanese Corporate System*, London, Kegan Paul, 1991.
Morgan, James C., and Morgan, Jeffrey J., *Cracking The Japanese Market*, New York, Free Press, 1991.
Morita, Akio, *Made in Japan, Akio Morita and Sony*, New York, E.P. Dutton, 1986.
Odaka, Kunio, *Japanese Management—A Forward-Looking Analysis*, Tokyo, Asian Productivity Organization, 1986.
Ouchi, William, *Theory Z*, Reading, Addison-Wesley, 1981.
Pascale, Richard Tanner, and Athos, Anthony G., *The Art of Japanese Management*, New York, Simon & Schuster, 1981.

Sato, Kazuo, and Hoshino, Yasuo, *The Anatomy of Japanese Business*, Armonk, M.E. Sharpe, 1984.

Sethi, S. Prakash, Namiki, Nobuaki, and Swanson, Carl L., *The False Promise of the Japanese Miracle*, Boston, Pitman, 1984

Small and Medium Enterprise Agency, *White Paper on Small and Medium Enterprises in Japan*, Tokyo, annual.

Smitka, Michael J., *Competitive Ties, Subcontracting in the Japanese Automotive Industry*, Princeton, Princeton University Press.

3. Industrial Relations

Chalmers, Norma J., *Industrial Relations in Japan, The Peripheral Workforce*, London, Routledge, 1989.

Clark, Rodney, *The Japanese Company*, New Haven, Yale University Press, 1979.

Cole, Robert E., *Japanese Blue Collar: The Changing Tradition*, Berkeley, University of California Press, 1971.

————, *Work, Mobility, and Participation*, Berkeley, University of California Press, 1979.

Dore, Ronald P., *British Factory, Japanese Factory*, Berkeley, University of California Press, 1973.

Hanami, Tadashi, *Labor Relations in Japan Today*, Tokyo, Kodansha International, 1979.

Kamata, Satoshi, *Japan In The Passing Lane*, New York, Pantheon, 1982.

Kawanishi, Hirosuke, *Enterprise Unionism in Japan*, London, Kegan Paul, 1991.

Koike, Kazuo, *Understanding Industrial Relations in Modern Japan*, New York, St. Martin's, 1988.

Levine, Solomon B., and Kawada, Hisashi, *Human Resources in Japanese Industrial Development*, Princeton, Princeton University Press, 1991.

Lincoln, James R, and Kalleberg, Arne L., *Culture, Control and Commitment*, Cambridge, Cambridge University Press, 1990.

Rohlen, Thomas P., *For Harmony And Strength*, Berkeley, University of California Press, 1974.

Schonberger, Richard J., *Japanese Manufacturing Techniques*, New York, Free Press, 1982.

Sengoku, Tamotsu, *Willing Workers: The Work Ethic in Japan, England, and the United States*, Westport, Quorum, 1985.

Shirai, Taishiro (ed.), *Contemporary Industrial Relations in Japan*, Madison, University of Wisconsin Press, 1983.

Taira, Koji, *Economic Development and the Labor Market in Japan*, New York, Columbia University Press, 1968.

Woronoff, Jon, *Japan's Wasted Workers*, Tokyo, Yohan, and New York, Rowman and Allenheld, 1981.

4. Women Workers

Cook, Alice, and Hayashi, Hiroko, *Working Women in Japan: Discrimination, Resistance, and Reform*, Ithaca, Cornell University Press, 1980.

Kondo, Dorinne K., *Crafting Selves*, Chicago, University of Chicago Press, 1990.

Lo, Jeannie, *Office Ladies, Factory Women*, Armonk, M.E. Sharpe, 1990.

Ministry of Labor, *White Paper on Women's Labor*, Tokyo, annual.

Saso, Mary, *Women in the Japanese Workplace*, London, Hilary Shipman, 1990.

5. Cultural, Social, Political

Alletzhauser, Albert J., *The House of Nomura*, New York, Harper, 1990.

Calder, Kent E., *Crisis and Compensation*, Princeton, Princeton University Press, 1988.

Economic Planning Agency, *White Paper on National Life*, Tokyo, annual.

Fukutake, Tadashi, *Japanese Society Today*, Tokyo, University of Tokyo Press, 1981.

————, *The Japanese Social Structure*, Tokyo, University of Tokyo Press, 1982.

Hidaka, Rokuro, *The Price of Affluence*, Tokyo, Kodansha International, 1984.

Holstein, William J., *The Japanese Power Game*, New York, Scribners, 1990.

Johnson, Chalmers, *MITI And The Japanese Miracle*, Stanford, Stanford University Press, 1982.

Kumori, Shumpei, and Rosovsky, Henry, *The Political Economy of Japan: Cultural and Social Dynamics*, Stanford, Stanford University Press, 1992.

Ministry of Labor, *Survey of Japanese Employees' Life After Retirement*, Tokyo, annual.

Prime Minister's Office, *Public Opinion Survey on Society and State*, Tokyo, annual.

————, *Public Opinion Survey on The Life of The Nation*, Tokyo, annual.

Taylor, Jared, *Shadows of the Rising Sun*, New York, Quill, 1983.

van Wolferen, Karel, *The Enigma of Japanese Power*, New York, Knopf, 1989.

Vogel, Ezra, *Japan As Number One*, Cambridge, Harvard University Press, 1988.

Woronoff, Jon, *Asia's "Miracle" Economies*, 2nd edition, Armonk, M.E. Sharpe, 1991.

————, *Japan As—Anything But—Number One*, London, Macmillan, and Armonk, M.E. Sharpe, 1991.

————, *Japan: The Coming Social Crisis*, Tokyo, Yohan, 1983.

————, *Politics, The Japanese Way*, London, Macmillan, and New York, St. Martin's, 1988.

Yamamura, Kozo, *Japan's Economic Structure: Should It Change?*, Society for Japanese Studies, Seattle, 1990.

Index

Abegglen, James, 207, 209
administrative reform, 54, 97
advanced countries, 25, 37, 76, 127, 141–2, 206, 227–8
agriculture, 67–8, 76, 78, 88–9, 92, 100, 123
aid, 34, 36–7
airlines, 121, 124
Allen, Deborah, 101
amenities, 131–2, 224–5
Arai, Joji, 72
Asia, 29, 76, 101, 104, 223–4
automation, 80, 112
automobile industry, 49, 90, 121, 177–9

Bank of Japan, 38, 41, 51, 57, 237
banks, 50–1, 66, 90, 122, 199, 201
birth rate, 28, 138, 144
Blinder, Alan, 110, 210–1
Board of Audit, 96–7
bubble economy, 31–2, 51–2, 122–3
bureaucrats, 40–1, 45–9, 57–8, 92–7, 110, 124, 214–6, 231–4
businessmen, 45–9, 50–4, 94–5, 97, 214–6, 231–4
Business Week, 24, 104

Chalmers, Norma, 72
companies, 68–72, 204–12, *see also* management
company "family," 79–80, 155–60, 169–74
competition, 106–8, 113, 118, 122, 176
construction, 65–6, 77–8, 91–2, 123–4
consumers, 90, 115–20, 121–3, 163–5, 220, 226
core system, 173–4, 208, 212
corruption, 52, 125, 197, 199, 201
cost of living, 26, 66–8, 88–9, 100–1, 112, 115–21, 129

credit cards, 31, 164–5
crisis, 11–22, 219–41

debt, personal, 164–5; national, 53–4, 97
decision-making, 82, 87–8, 232–3
declining sectors, 29–30, 40, 65, 108, 121
defense, 34, 36, 96
Dentsu Institute of Human Studies, 163
deregulation, 51, 57, 96, 122
distribution, 55, 66–7, 77–8, 89–90, 92, 96, 117–20, 123, 171
Doko, Toshiwo, 54
domestic demand, 30–1, 40–1, 57–8, 226
Dore, Ronald, 36, 174, 179
Drucker, Peter, 40
dual economy, 70–2, 77

Economic Planning Agency (EPA), 23, 45–8, 128, 140, 165, 195
Economist, 40–1, 45, 58, 229
education, 26, 83–4, 86, 95, 131, 205, 213–4
Emmott, Bill, 55, 58, 127, 140, 229
endaka (heavy yen), 30–1, 38, 57, 234
Equal Employment Opportunity Law, 186–7
Europe, 25, 27, 33–4, 36–9, 55–8, 76–8, 88, 99–101, 104, 111, 123,
    131, 142, 189, 202, 206, 223, 231
exchange rates, 30–1, 38, 58, 99, 109, 117, 123, 233
exporting, 17, 29, 35–6, 38, 54–5, 57–8, 109, 226, 229, 233–4

Fair Trade Commission (FTC), 118–9
family, 137, 143, 150, 162, 164–6, 189–90
finance, 66, 78, 122–3
Financial Times, 24, 39
Fiscal Investment and Loan Program (FILP), 53
fiscal policy, 52–4
food costs, 100, 117, 123
Fukuda, Takeo, 214

generation gap, 138, 150–3, 159–66, 226–7
geographic gaps, 16, 203–4
Germany, 26, 33–4, 100, 104, 111, 114, 133, 180, 191, 206, 222–3
Gibney, Frank, 149–50
Great Britain, 100, 104, 114, 207, 223
Gregory, Gene, 155
growth, 11, 14–6, 23–6, 32–7, 47–8, 78, 99, 219–20, 224–6, 228, 238

Hakuhodo Institute of Life, 162
Hasegawa, Keitaro, 159

Hayashi, Hikaru, 162
health care, 141–2
hierarchy, 83–4, 170–3, 196, 202–6, 208–9, 212–7, 232–1
Honda, 42, 49, 107
Hong Kong, 25, 39, 223
honne (reality), 19, 143, 153
hours worked, 79, 82–3, 96, 132–7, 176–8, 184
housing, 26, 100–1, 128–9, 132, 138, 142–3, 202–3

implosion, 22, 166, 235–6
income, 99–103, 164–5, 201
industrial policy, *see* targeting
inequality, 13, 16–7, 19, 51–2, 129, 195–217, 227–8
inflation, 25–7, 102, 112, 114
International Labour Organisation, 112
investment, 29, 41–2, 58–9, 109–10
Ishikawa, Rokuro, 153, 165

Japanapologists, 7–8, 20, 23, 37–42, 45, 55, 57–8, 71–2, 127, 149–50, 155, 174–5, 179, 223–4, 229, 240–1
Japan Chamber of Commerce and Industry, 153, 165
Japan Development Bank (JDB), 105, 238
Japan Economic Journal, 31, 119, 237
Japan Federation of Economic Organizations (Keidanren), 54
Japan Federation of Employers Associations (Nikkeiren), 114, 207
Japan Productivity Council (JPC), 76–7
job-hopping, 159–60, 163
Johnson, Chalmers, 45
journalists, 20, 24, 29, 39, 40, 229, 240

Kahn, Herman, 23, 32
Kalleberg, Arne L., 175–6
Kamata, Satoshi, 177–9
Kansai Economic Federation, 203–4
karoshi (death from overwork), 184–5
keiretsu (groups), 55, 170, 204
Kobayashi, Noritake, 110
Korea, 25, 29, 39, 56, 65, 128, 223
kudoka (hollowing), 29, 41
Kyocera, 49, 210

labor costs, 29, 76, 92, 227
Labor Department (U.S.), 111
labor force, 92, 95
land prices, 26, 30, 52, 101, 122–3, 132, 197–9, 213
leisure, 101, 112, 134–9, 203

Liberal Democratic Party (LDP), 93–4
"lifetime" employment, 85, 108, 111, 156–60, 170–3, 183–6, 188, 206
Lincoln, James R., 175–6
loan sharks, 66

Macrae, Norman, 45–6, 50
Maekawa Plans, 57–8, 229, 233
Management and Coordination Agency, 100, 128–9, 164
management system, 84–8, 104–10, 155–60, 169–92
manufacturing, 61–4, 76–8
market share, 105–9
Matsushita, 107, 210–1, 213, 215
middle-class consciousness, 196–7, 203–4
Ministry of Agriculture, 88, 95–6
Ministry of Finance (MOF), 45, 50–4, 95–6, 122–3
Ministry of Health, 121
Ministry of International Trade and Industry (MITI), 45, 47–50, 57, 65,
    71, 95–6, 109, 117–8, 120, 146
Ministry of Labor, 132, 180, 184
Ministry of Post and Telecommunications, 49, 121
Ministry of Transport, 49, 121
monetary policy, 51–2
Morgan, James & Jeffrey, 169
Morita, Akio, 112, 195

Nakasone, Yasuhiro, 46–7, 54, 57, 215
Nakatani, Iwao, 104, 110
NEC, 107
nepotism, 214–5
Nevins, Thomas J., 169
newly industrialized countries (NICs), 25, 55, 72, 76
Nihon Keizai Shimbun, see Japan Economic Journal
Nippon Telegraph and Telephone (NTT), 121–2, 124
Nixon shock, 29, 38
Nomura, 200

Occupation, 33–4
Odaka, Kunio, 85–6, 157–8, 181
Organization of Economic Cooperation and Development (OECD), 37,
    76–7, 206
office ladies (OLs), 83, 89–90, 203
Ohta, Hajime, 81
oil crises, 30, 37–8, 65
old age, 140–8, 185–6, 206, 233
Osano, Kenji, 213

Ouchi, William, 155
overtime, 79, 112–3, 133

people, 97, 102–3, 119–20, 202–4, 217, 221–2, 228, 231–2, 234–5
petrochemicals, 37, 49, 65, 121
planning, 45–8
Plaza Accord, 38, 57
politicians, 92–4, 97, 110, 124–5, 145–6, 201–2, 214–5, 231–4, 237–8
Prime Minister's Office, 134, 180, 237
productivity, 33, 62, 69, 72, 75–84, 88, 107, 112, 176–8
profitability, 69–70, 91, 104–10, 122
protectionism, foreign, 56, 226; Japanese, 55–6, 68, 116–7, 120
public opinion polls, 21, 128, 134–5, 137–8, 140–1, 152, 160, 161–2,
    164, 180–1, 184–5, 191–2, 195–6, 236–7
public works, 51, 53, 124–5, 132, 225

quality control, 63, 79–82, 133, 177–8, 189
quality of life, 127–47

railways, 53, 97, 121, 124, 129–30
Recruit, 160
Rengo, 101
revisionism, 7–8

salaryman, 19, 81–3, 136–8, 151–2, 172, 179–86
Sasaki, Hajime, 107
savings, 50–1, 142, 164–5
scandals, 52, 197, 200
social security, 54, 142–6
services, 66–7, 90–2, 225–6
Shimomura, Osamu, 38–9
shipbuilding, 26, 65
shokku (shocks), 28–32, 37
Singapore, 25, 223
Small and Medium Enterprise Agency, 70–1
small companies, 69–72, 77, 151, 204–6
Sony, 42, 49, 107, 112, 195
Stalk, George, 207
standard of living, 12, 100, 238
statistics, 13, 25–8, 33, 100, 103, 220
stock market, 30, 41, 52, 122, 198–201
subcontracting, 70–1, 77, 91, 157
Sugahara, Mariko, 164
Suzuki, Zenko, 214

Taiwan, 25, 39, 56, 65, 223
Takahashi, Nobuaki, 238

Takeda, Kunitaro, 88
Takeshita, Noburo, 54, 215
targeting, 47–50, 62, 65, 71, 116, 120–3, 220
tatemae (illusion), 19, 143, 150, 153
taxes, 53–4, 201–2, 213, 216, 225
technology, 35–6
Tokyo, 18–9, 93, 100, 129, 203–4, 214
Towers Perrin, 207
Toyo Keizai, 88, 207
Toyota, 110, 176–9, 215
trade friction, 17, 29–30, 36, 38–9, 54–9, 226, 228

unemployment, 27–8, 113, 156
United Nations, 186
United States, 26–7, 29–30, 33–6, 38–9, 53, 55–9, 68, 76–8, 88, 93,
  99–101, 104, 114–5, 128, 131, 133, 142, 175–6, 180, 191, 202, 206–
  7, 224, 231

Van Wolferen, Karel, 230
Vogel, Ezra, 155, 169

wages, 111–5, 155, 158–9, 164, 179, 183, 186, 197, 205–7, 227
Wall Street Journal, 29
welfare, 12, 17, 28, 95, 113, 140–7, 225
women, 81–3, 90, 112–3, 137–8, 157, 164, 172–3, 186–92, 205–6, 208,
  235
worker, blue-collar, 79–81, 172, 174–80, 189–90, 205; peripheral, 113,
  142, 156–7, 171–3, 204–6, 212; white-collar, 77–88, 172, 179–86,
  189–90, 205, 208
work will, 149–60, 227
World Bank, 34

Yamaha, 107, 181
yen, 29–31, *see also* exchange rates
Yomiuri Shimbun, 102, 134
youth, 161–5, 180, 183, 231, 233–5